When the Northern Lights Went Dark

My Journey through Loss and Grief to Healing and Hope

Rev. Dr. Brian L. Erickson
brianerickson50@gmail.com
Blog: *Meandering Spirituality*
www.pastorbrianerickson.blogspot.com

*Master of Divinity and
Doctor of Ministry*
**Luther Theological Seminary,
Saint Paul, MN**

The Northern Lights picture on the cover was taken
by
Markus Trienke and posted in Wikimedia
Commons,
and is used with permission:
https://flickr.com/photos/102769624@N02/169154
32661

The poem quoted at the beginning of each chapter
of Part II is by Kahlil Gibran, "The Life of Love,"
Tears and Laughter (New York: The Philosophical
Library, Inc., 1949), pp. 22-24.

The Dan Fogelberg lyric quotations at the
beginning of chapters in Part III are from his album,
"The Innocent Age."

The drawing of Pauline in Chapter 6 is by John R.
Nyberg.

Dedication I

This book is dedicated to Edrei Arnold and Ruth Lois, who gave me life and filled that life with such love and joy in the short years we had together. It is also dedicated to Pauline Marie, who filled my life with joy, love and grace, and demonstrated how life can be lived in faith, trust and hope in the face of great suffering and the possibility of death. These three showed me that love is, indeed, eternal.

Acknowledgments

I am extremely grateful to the following persons who read all or parts of the manuscript, and made many helpful suggestions: Craig McEwen, Mary Guttormson Erickson, Jessi Erickson, Margaret Ann Haukness Horstmann, Alan Erickson, Tim Thorstenson, Judy Wick Dodge, Julie Tweit, Jerry Pyle, Lisa and Lanny Faleide, Joel Gilbertson, Bill and Joel Raaen, Elmo and Norma Anderson, Dana Dreibelbis.

A special thank you goes to Ellen Webber for extensive suggestions on content and organization.

Thank you to Brian J. Erickson for assistance with the cover design.

Contents

Part I The Search for One's Self

Part II   Seasons of Life and Love

Part III   The Long Journey Home

Part I

The Search for One's Self

Introduction

It is not our job to remain whole.
We came to lose our leaves
Like the trees, and be born again,
Drawing up from the great roots.
— **Robert Bly**

How do we know who we are? How do we know what has made us who we are?

If events in our lives had happened differently, even slightly differently, would we be different than who we are today?

Whoever we think we are, are we content with that? Have we made peace with that? Can we live, even happily, and perhaps joyfully, with whoever we are today? Or however we understand who we are today?

These are not easy questions to answer. And, even when we do, we never know for sure if the answers are correct.

However, that is not really important. A lot of life is about correctness, but the journey to understand who we are, and why we are that way, is not really about correctness. It is about persistence, about being open to life (with all its ambiguities) and about asking God and others for support and direction. Finally, it is about living in grace, accepting life as it has unfolded for us, and rejoicing in the forgiveness and love that is all around us, every day, if we can only open our eyes and hearts to it.

My life has been shaped by loss. Losses, at an early age, from death. Grief is our response to loss, and I have done a lot of grieving in my life. A lot of that grieving has been hidden, but eventually I learned how to be more open about it. I also learned there are places where it will be accepted and soothed, and places where it will not be accepted and you will feel like your very soul has been violated.

I have no doubt that these losses, and the grieving I have done, have shaped who I am and how I see life and the world.

My psychological journey has taken me through guilt, anger, rage, loneliness and despair to comfort, healing and hope. By the way, that is not a straight-line journey: it's more like a merry-go-round on which you try to learn how to enjoy the ride, even though it keeps making you feel sick from time to time.

My losses have also shaped how I see God and how I understand the spiritual journey. God and I--and the church and I--have had a lot of struggles over the years. It took me a long time to finally understand that God and our theologies about God are not the same. Sometimes we may even be ready to give up God before we give up our theologies. Thank God that my spiritual journey eventually got to the point where I was able to change my theology so that I could finally experience the healing, love and hope God always wants to give us.

I have just observed the 41st anniversary of my ordination as a pastor in the Lutheran church (the Evangelical Lutheran in America, to be exact). That journey has taken me from a little town of 700 people in North Dakota—Maddock—where I was raised for 18 years, to education, teaching, and pastoral ministry in Moorhead, Minnesota, Chicago; Minneapolis/St. Paul; Boston; Spokane; Fargo; Hemet, California; Mexico; Switzerland; Phoenix; and the greater Washington D.C. area.

I have experienced love and grace over and over again throughout my life, but that experience of love has come through and along with much pain and struggle. I have been shaped by loss and grief, and by the God and communities of love who bore me when I could not walk myself.

In what follows I share the losses that have shaped me, and what I have learned from them, not so that you can get to know me, but so that you can get to know yourself. I believe that the most particular is also the most universal, and that my story will lead you deeper into your own story as you try to understand who you are and why you are the way you are. As you do that, I am pretty sure that you will love yourself even more.

Prologue   Graves

I bequeath myself to the dirt to grow from the grass I love,
If you want me again look for me under your boot-soles.

Failing to fetch me at first keep encouraged,
Missing me one place search another,
I stop somewhere waiting for you.
  -- Walt Whitman, "Song of Myself"

"Hello Mom. Hello Dad. It has been a long time."

I was standing over Mom's and Dad's graves. How long had it been? So many years! How could that be? Where had those years gone?

I was there not to say goodbye, but to say hello. Hello so that I could tell Dad and Mom about Pauline, the love of my life, whom they had never met.

Graves are such strange places. We stay away from them at all costs, sure that they will increase our pain and sense of loss. Just as folks have the mistaken notion that if they don't mention our loss, we won't feel it so deeply, we tend to believe that if we can just stay away from those graves, our pain will be less severe.

But it doesn't work that way. When it comes to our losses, and the grief those losses create, our healing and hope for the future can only come through facing the pain head on, and walking straight through it, hopefully with the love and support of many caring people.

When your parents die when they are young, and you are also, every future celebration, no matter how glorious, carries a kind of emptiness. You want them to be there for your graduations. And they are not. You want them to be there for your wedding. And they are not. You want them to be there for your ordination into ministry. And they are not. You want them to be there for the birth of your children. And they are not. You want them to be there for your children's baptisms, and graduations, and weddings, and they are not.

Graves, strangely, can become a place of healing, not because our loved ones are actually there, but because the earthen place in which their ashes lie can become a sacred ground upon which we can bring together our losses and loves to meet each other. As such, graves can become a place of insight, revelation, reconciliation, forgiveness, healing and renewed hope.

"Mom! Dad! You never met Pauline, but, if you had, you would love her very much. And she loves you very much."

The graves I stood over are in North Viking Lutheran Cemetery in Maddock, North Dakota, a rural community almost exactly in the center of that prairie state. This is where I lived until leaving to attend Concordia College in Moorhead, Minnesota, in the year of our Lord, 1968. It was in the fall of that year, as a pimple-faced freshman, that I met Pauline.

The school year hadn't even started. I was there for freshmen orientation, which included making all of us wear little, yellow, round caps, called "beanies," just to make sure everyone knew who the frosh were so that they could be kept in their place.

It was time for supper (which is what we call the last meal of the day in the Midwest) and I was standing with the other frosh, and the football players who had arrived even earlier to begin practice, waiting for the doors of the Commons, our campus cafeteria, to open. This was the favorite place of students on campus where, in addition to eating our meals, we bought snacks, shot pool and occasionally had entertainment, like the time John Denver showed up to play his guitar and sing about country roads.

My eyes fell upon another frosh who was walking towards the Commons with a bunch of other young women. Asking around, I was told that she was Pauline Peterson from Bismarck, North Dakota.

Coming from a small, rural town like Maddock, I didn't know if I had the courage to ask out a young woman from a big city (by North Dakota standards) like Bismarck, or Grand Forks, or Fargo, let alone the Twin Cities of Minneapolis/St. Paul, which sent an amazing number of students to the hinterlands of Minnesota.

However, during the next few days I kept an eye out for Pauline and finally, in early September, I got up the courage to go up to her in the Commons and ask her if she wanted to have coffee sometime. When she said yes, I almost jumped out of my shoes.

I was totally smitten. Pauline was petite, 5" 4", and just barely over a hundred pounds. She had gorgeous, brown eyes and long, dark hair. Her outward beauty was matched by a beauty of spirit. She had a mysterious kind of presence: quiet and gentle, yet you could see the passion in her eyes. She spoke little, smiled easily, loved to laugh and felt life deeply.

Concordia in those days was fairly parochial. No alcohol or dancing was allowed on campus. It was also sexist. While men could smoke on campus and had no hours, women could not smoke and had a curfew each night. Even on weekend nights women had to be back in their dorms by 10 pm.

However, Pauline and I devised a plan whereby she could stay out later. She would lightly knock on her dorm window and her roommate, Mary, would take off the window screen so Pauline could crawl back into her room.

Pauline and I had a few dates, leading up to a Friday night in the middle of the fall on which there was a dance at an off-campus venue. Pauline and I made plans to attend.

One of my buddies from Red Willow Bible Camp (where I had worked three summers during high school), Duey Lura, was coming down from Mayville State University to spend the weekend with me, including going to the dance. That afternoon I got a phone call from Pauline telling me she could not join me. I don't recall the reason she gave, but I remember being so upset that I took quarters out of my pocket and began tossing them down the dorm corridor.

Duey arrived, I was bummed I could not show Pauline off to him, but we decided to go to the dance anyway. When we arrived I spotted Pauline. She was there with another guy! Just like in the movies! Talk about an ego-buster!

I tried my best to ignore her, but not Duey. While Pauline and this other guy were dancing a typical 1960's dance, where you were a few feet apart, doing the Twist or some such step, Duey walked between them and glared at Pauline. Well, I thought, I guess this is what buddies are for.

This whole episode was not particularly helpful to my self-confidence. Yes, it was another loss, but one not nearly as painful as the losses I had already experienced in life. And, two and a half years later, Pauline and I would meet again, and this time it would be much different.

However—before we get to that—how did I come to be standing over the graves of both of my parents, who had died, less than two years apart, before I had turned seventeen?

Chapter 1   Dad

In a barren and unhappy time I wanted to share
with my father the burden of my losses,
not the least of which was his grievous absence.
— **Stanley Kunitz, "The Poet's Quest for the Father"**

"How long have you known about this?" It wasn't the words that woke me. It was my mother's voice being raised, which I had seldom heard. My parents were eating breakfast in the nook off the kitchen next to where my brother and I had our bedrooms. I would only find out later what my mom was talking about, and I would only find out much later how that morning would change both the direction and the nature of my life.

It was September of 1964, and I had just celebrated my 14th birthday. My dad had noticed a growth beside his right ear. Like many people, and especially men, he had ignored it in hopes that it "would just go away." The growth would turn out to be a malignant cancer, which Dad would have removed surgically that fall. So began our journey with cancer, and a radical change in the near-perfect life I had been living up until that beautiful, fall morning.

We were living in the small, farming community of Maddock, North Dakota. We had two wonderful parents who loved us in every way possible. My father taught history and was the principal at our high school. My mother stayed at home to raise my older brother, Neil (at 9 years older, he had already graduated from college and begun his first job in Chicago), my younger brother, Alan, who was two grades below me in school and me.

I adored my dad, who was always present at all of our athletic and musical activities and played with us nearly constantly. Our neighbors, the Hauknesses, complained that they often had sore necks from watching various balls be thrown back and forth in our front yard. In the fall it was a football. In the spring and summer it was baseball. In the summer we could also be found at the schoolyard basketball court that my dad and other men in the community had built.

In the fall Dad took us hunting for Sharp-tailed grouse, Hungarian partridge and pheasants. And then there was golf. My dad, who loved to play whenever he could, especially with his best friend from across the street, Ansel Haukness, had taught me the game at an early age. I played with Dad and Alan often, and on other days my dad or mom would drop me at the course on a summer morning and I would play the whole day by myself or with my buddies.

When I wasn't at school I was at our church, North Viking Lutheran. I sang in the youth choir, always attended worship and Sunday School with my parents and, during the week, went to the church for Cub Scouts or junior choir.

Until that September morning in 9th grade, other than the usual ups and downs of growing up, my life had pretty much been wonderful. The only negatives I experienced were in grade school where I got mostly B's in my classes and C's in Conduct, both of which did not entirely please my parents, who felt I was capable of much better. The C's in Conduct were mainly from talking too much in class.

The only traumatic experience I had had was in 5th or 6th grade. My buddy, Billy Gorrie, and I got in a fight with another student in the schoolyard playground. He had told what we considered to be a lie about us, which could "get us in trouble" (as we used to say) with our parents and teachers. Billy and I responded by confronting the student and roughing him up just a little bit. That evening the boy's father tracked Billy and me down and verbally attacked us regarding our actions, with the father looking me straight in the eyes and yelling, "Erickson, you are nothing but a hood, and you will never amount to anything!"

There are some things said to us throughout life that we remember exactly as they were said, word for word. This was the first time that happened to me.

However, all of these negatives were turned around in junior high. In 7th and 8th grade I had two wonderful teachers who took it upon themselves to push me academically and to improve my behavior. The result was that I started getting all A's in my classes and also in my behavior, now graded as Self Conduct.

The other blessing occurred during that time frame in church. I began confirmation classes with a retired pastor whom I found to be quite boring. He was filling in for our church's pastor who had moved to another town. Then, in 8th grade, a new pastor came to our church, Elmo W Anderson, who radically changed the trajectory of my life, and is my mentor to this day.

My spiritual transition began in Pastor Elmo's confirmation classes, where I would first experience the part of the spiritual journey that leads from ritual and the head to emotion and the heart. My two best buddies in those years were Billy Gorrie and Joel Raaen (both of whom would move away from Maddock before high school—to my great sadness). This was Pastor Elmo's second pastoral call, and to this day he loves to tell the story of how surprised and delighted he was to encounter at North Viking three boys who loved to ask challenging questions. And we did.

We had already experienced the ritual part of faith: regularly attending worship, Sunday School and Vacation Bible School. Now we had the opportunity to experience the head part in an atmosphere in which we were not only allowed to ask the hard questions of faith, but were actually encouraged to do so.

On the more conservative side of Christianity doubt is considered to be the antithesis of faith. On the more progressive side it is considered to be an aspect of faith as we genuinely struggle with not only what we are supposed to believe, but also with what we actually do believe.

Even more importantly, Pastor Elmo helped us move from the head to the heart by taking us to Red Willow Bible Camp each summer for a week of camp. During that week I experienced a deepening of faith through small group discussion with trained college counselors and through skits, music and campfire singing with testimonials and worship and preaching geared to the situation of adolescents. I loved camp so much that during the summer after my 8th grade year I actually attended camp for a second week with kids from an entirely different area of the state. This involvement in both church and Bible camping pleased Mom and Dad, both of whom were deeply serious about their faith and very involved in our congregation.

My dad was a complicated man: an intriguing combination of sternness, playfulness, dedication, compassion, faith and humor. He was born Edrei Arnold Erickson in Francis, Saskatchewan on August 19, 1911, the seventh child in a family of nine children. His father was from Minnesota and his mother was an immigrant from Norway. His parents had moved to Canada to homestead in 1903, and then returned to the United States in 1918 to take up farming in North Dakota. Dad became a U.S. citizen at age 14.

Dad was intelligent and athletic. His family was pretty much dirt-poor, and thus when he graduated from high school there was no money to send him to college. However, he received a partial scholarship to play baseball at Wheaton College, located 25 miles west of Chicago. Wheaton is a conservative, Christian university, started in the 1853 by Wesleyan Methodists, which was the church tradition in which both my mom and dad were raised. Wheaton is also the school from which Billy Graham, Jr. graduated, having arrived on campus some 3 years after my dad.

Dad apparently had a fairly active social life at Wheaton. His 1937 annual, the Wheaton College Tower, is filled with notes from classmates. A number of the students referred to him as "Swede," even though he was almost totally Norwegian. A student named Helga wrote: "Best wishes to the gorgeous virtuoso."

And Carol wrote: "To the handsome Senior Romeo whose gallant smile cheers the world which vibrates at each complement he donates."

Dad drove an Eddy's bread truck to support his education, but even that did not provide enough funding. One day at the beginning of his senior year he was called into the financial office and confronted with the fact that he was behind in paying his expenses. When he explained that he had no more money, the financial aid officer suggested he write home for support. "Write home for money?" Dad responded. "My parents are writing me for money!"

"Well, then," the officer continued, "I'm afraid you are going to need to leave school." "That's too bad," Dad replied. "I was really looking forward to my senior year on the baseball team." "Oh, you are on the team? Well, I didn't realize that. I'm sure we can make some accommodation." It was thus that Dad was able to graduate from college with a B.A. major in Sociology and a minor in History on August 7, 1936.

Meanwhile, Dad had met a young woman named Ruth Lois Brown (born December 29, 1917) from Steele, North Dakota, the third youngest child of a dozen kids of a Methodist minister, Herbert Brown (and Lora). When Dad could secure a car he would drive the eleven miles from his hometown of Driscoll, beside the Burlington Northern railroad tracks, to Steele to court Mom. Dorothy, one of Mom's sisters, loved to tell of how Dad would keep driving around the block trying to muster the courage to actually ring the doorbell. I don't know if he was afraid of being met by Pastor Brown, or too shy to ask Mom for another date, or concerned that he might be seen as "robbing the cradle," (he was 6 years older than Mom), but he admitted he loved it when Dorothy answered the door, because she was exceedingly kind and hospitable.

Edrei and Ruth were married in Rugby, North Dakota by Mom's father on her 20th birthday, December 29, 1937. Their first son, my older brother Neil, was born four years later to the day.

Dad began a series of small town teaching jobs across North Dakota. During the summers he worked for Anderson

Furniture Store in Rugby, where his father-in-law was serving as a pastor. Eventually Anderson's opened another store in Maddock, and Dad was asked to manage it (along with the accompanying funeral business). Dad was ready for a change from teaching and accepted the offer in 1944. My folks moved to the apartment at the back of the store and settled in to the business that Dad would eventually buy from the Andersons.

It was while Mom and Dad were living in that small apartment that I was born on August 30, 1950. My earliest memories are of playing with our dog and running around the furniture in the store, constantly being chided not to damage anything.

Eventually my parents built a house on the east side of town and, whenever I hear the term "home," I think of that house. Alan was born a year and a half after me, and thus, even after Neil grew up and left home, Dad still had two boys to play with and guide.

Dad was a great storyteller and had a wonderful sense of humor, which I first witnessed as he visited with customers in the store. His best friend, Ansel Haukness, was also a great storyteller. Between the two of them there was always plenty of banter and laughter, including chiding from their wives for telling the same stories over and over again, and challenges as to what was really the truth. But, as Ansel liked to say, "Do you want the truth or do you want it interesting?"

Eventually it became harder to make a living with a furniture store in a small town, and in 1958 Dad decided to return to teaching. He secured a teaching position in Dilworth, Minnesota, just across the river from Fargo. I still remember riding the train to Fargo so we could look at possible houses in Dilworth. However, when folks got wind of this in Maddock, the high school administrators jumped into action and a teaching position was found at the high school so that our family could remain in Maddock.

In order to return to teaching, Dad had to take some classes, and so he spent that summer in Fargo studying at Moorhead State Teachers College. Our old Pontiac was on its last legs, and Dad went looking for a new car. He decided on one at Russ Buick in Fargo, a 1958 pink Buick Special. Oh, I still remember the day he drove that luxurious vehicle into our driveway. All the chrome in the front, the big fins on the back, power transmission and steering and a really fine radio. That fall Dad painted our house pink to match.

I loved this change in plans, and not only because we would not have to move. It also meant that Dad, not having to work the long hours in the store, including Saturdays, and having summers off, would have even more time to spend with us boys. By sixth grade I was old enough to take gun safety courses, and that meant that now I could not only accompany Dad when hunting, but I could hunt beside him. Dad gave me his Winchester Model 12 16-gauge, which he had gotten from his father. He told me that once someone had driven over the barrel with a pickup, but it had been straightened out and should shoot accurately. What was nice about this was that whenever I missed a shot—which happened a lot—I could always blame it on the gun.

Dad also had a warm, compassionate, caring side to him. Although I remember a few times when he was angry with me, most of the time he was gentle and caring. He never missed worship at church, and served on various church committees. Bill Raaen (the high school music teacher and father of one of my best friends, Joel) told me recently of a time when there had been a car accident east of Maddock that involved high school students. Dad asked Bill to go out with him to the site of the crash, and Bill related how profoundly moved Dad had been about what had happened, and they then discussed how they might most helpfully respond as teachers to the students involved.

Later there was another car accident south of Maddock in which one of Dad's high school students was killed. It had happened on quite a sharp curve in the road. I remember Dad showing that turn to Alan and me, and explaining why you really need to slow down when such a curve is coming up, especially at night.

All in all, my life seemed nearly perfect! However, all of that began to change with a growth under Dad's right ear that had begun to affect his hearing, and thus had finally elicited a confession to Mom about his having ignored a dangerous symptom.

Fortunately for me, I already had a fairly strong, spiritual basis when I heard that fateful question from my mother as I began high school in the ninth grade. But I would also hear that question as a fairly insecure adolescent, not ready to have my world turned upside down. And, like most kids that age, I took the path of least resistance, that of living in denial, which would lead to repressed guilt, with which I would struggle for over a decade before I would be able to bring it into consciousness so that it could finally be healed.

Trying not to dwell on Dad's illness, I threw myself into study, sports and the youth group at church. That fall I played football for the first time, as that sport was fairly new to our community. Because of our small school enrollment, the Maddock Bobcats joined a 9-man football conference (normally football teams have eleven players on the field at any given time). I played right end on offense, and left end on defense. I would also become our team's punter and kick off specialist.

Dad had his surgery to remove the tumor that fall, which left the left side of his face quite disfigured (which bothered him a great deal). He then began a long period of cobalt radiation treatments, which meant someone had to drive him back and forth the 140 miles one-way to Bismarck. Sometimes Mom took him, sometimes a relative, sometimes Pastor Elmo, sometimes his best friend Ansel, sometimes other members of the community. I really don't remember much about my feelings during those months—like I said, I was in denial, part of which means not exploring what is really going on right before your very eyes. Since Dad was constantly going to some kind of treatments, I hoped that medical science would provide a cure. Beyond that, I trusted spiritually that God would provide a way through, although I had no idea what exactly that would be.

Eventually, when he felt well enough to do so, Dad returned to teaching. I wish I could remember more clearly that one year we were in the same school building together. All I can remember is being in study hall when he was the monitor and seeing a bit of the dry humor that had a part in making him so beloved to his students.

That winter I played my favorite sport, basketball, starting on the junior varsity and also making the varsity, which took second in the Class B State Basketball Tournament. Dad was not well enough to travel to the tournament in Minot (110 miles away), but I have a picture of him greeting each team member at a special ceremony to welcome us home.

The following spring (and I don't remember whether I had discussed this with my parents ahead of time) I applied for and was accepted to be a Counselor in Training at Red Willow Bible Camp. Mom encouraged me to stay home to spend the summer with Dad. I remember (wishful thinking?) that Dad thought camp would be very good for me and that I should go. Later that summer I would come to understand why he felt that way.

The school year ended and off I went to orientation at camp. I was so thrilled to arrive and begin working with the counselors I had gotten to know during my three weeks at camp the previous two summers, and to start getting to know and work with peers, many of whom are still friends to this day.

Working at camp had an even more profound effect on my faith. As I studied the Bible more deeply, had conversations with other staff and various pastors about their faith journeys and heard many fine pastors preach, my commitment to God and the gospel continued to grow and strengthen.

Looking back I can see that at that point in my faith journey I had a fairly simplistic, conservative view of faith. It had started with what my mom taught me growing up, been confirmed in Sunday School and confirmation and deepened at Bible camp. I interpreted the Scriptures quite literally and saw whatever happened as somehow being God's will.

I therefore viewed Dad's illness as God's will, and thus as something I needed to find a way to accept, whether I liked it or not. My task was to be "strong in faith," no matter what happened, which also meant I wasn't encouraged to share my struggles in a very open way. The positive side of this kind of conservative theology is that one may find strength in believing that somehow, even if not understood, God is behind whatever is happening. The weakness of this theology is that it may lead to a repression of what one actually believes and is feeling, and often anger at this God who is either causing one's suffering, or at least allowing it to happen. I did not understand it at the time, but that is exactly what was going on inside of me.

That summer I fell in love once or twice, made both male and female life-long friends, played lots of softball and basketball and experienced a deepening of my faith and a growing understanding of the importance of a loving, supportive Christian community. I also started teaching myself guitar so I could lead singing at our campfires. This new skill would evolve into a three-person group, modeled after Peter, Paul and Mary, to sing songs in worship and at neighboring churches on Sunday mornings.

Mom tried to write me letters fairly regularly, but that became more and more difficult as Dad's health deteriorated. The three things Mom and Dad wanted to know is if I had enough money, if I was finding a way to get my clothes washed and if I had gotten a haircut. I think they were afraid I might look like one of the Beatles.

Towards the end of June they wrote looking for a way to get me home the week of July 4, as Neil was coming home to visit. Mom ended her letter of June 26, "We are all anxious to see you and have you home again. It's been pretty quiet and lonesome here. Lovingly, Dad, Mother and Alan"

I decided to skip a Luther League Leadership Training School so that I could go home for that week.

As the summer passed, the cancerous tumor continued to grow larger, greatly disfiguring Dad's face. Even so, he continued to welcome visitors.

My next letter from Mom was on July 22. She wrote "Dad is looking forward to having you home in another two weeks. He says he is going to have you sit by him and talk to him and read to him." Dad could no longer see well enough to do his own reading. She ended the letter, "Continue to remember your dad in your prayers that his faith may remain strong as it is now and that God's Will be done. Lovingly, Dad and Mother. P.S. Do you need money?"

Dad had two lawn chairs made out of heavy steel, which in the summer he kept in the front of the house. There he would sit on summer days, waiting for people to stop by and sit down for an iced tea. Ansel could often be found there, and also Paul Haukness, who was home from college for the summer

Bill Raaen had left Maddock in 1963, at which point Dad had replaced him as principal. Bill returned in the summer of 1965 to visit Dad. As he walked toward our house, Dad yelled out: "Stop! You are not going to like what you see!" But Bill did stop to catch up on things, and it was during this return visit that Dad had told him how grateful he was to God for having given him that year to reflect on his life and deepen his relationship with God.

Dad had decided to use his battle with cancer as an opportunity to strengthen his spiritual journey. Spending many long hours alone, he read his Bible and devotional books. He listened to his favorite hymns, sung by George Beverly Shea. I think my older brother might even have gotten him a record of Elvis Presley singing gospel songs. That took a bit of adjustment by Dad, but he was hungry for the gospel wherever he could find it.

Early in August Mom called me at camp to tell me Dad was getting worse, and I needed to leave camp early and come home. At first I argued with her, saying I wanted to stay at camp. We had just completed a long summer of hosting campers, and now, at the end of the summer, the camp staff was going on a weeklong canoe trip down the Sheyenne River.

However, Mom would not be detoured. She told me to pack my bags and on Sunday, August 8, she drove to Red Willow and picked me up in Dad's pride and joy: his 1958 pink Buick Special.

When I got home I found that Dad could hardly eat anything and was restricted to bed. He called for me to come into his bedroom. He asked me to sit on the edge of the bed, and then he told me the story of his faith journey.

He said he had been quite serious about his faith growing up and especially when he was a student at Wheaton College. He then explained that, over the years, church had become something to belong to and be involved in, but he had not focused much on his relationship with God.

That had changed in the past year. Through Bible reading, listening to Christian music, having visits with Pastor Elmo and discussions with Mom, his faith had deepened again, and he had realized what he had been missing the past several years.

He talked about how he had often been asked to teach Sunday School, but had responded by saying that since he taught during the week he did not want to do the same on Sundays. Now, however, if he were to be healed he would not only teach Sunday School, but become much more involved in the ministry of the church.

Dad then explained that the reason he had supported me in going to Bible Camp was because he felt that experience would be important to my own faith journey.

I thanked Dad for letting me go to camp and told him of some of the deeply spiritual experiences I had had, and how I was beginning to think that maybe I should consider becoming a pastor.

As I look back on that conversation, two things amaze me. First, Dad never said anything that might make me feel guilty. He didn't say, "I really missed you this summer," or "I wish you had been at home more." That took tremendous discipline, because I am sure that is how he felt. However, I already felt plenty of repressed guilt, and Dad was gracious not to pile on.

Secondly, he did not try to elicit any promises about the future. He didn't say, 'Well, I am glad you are serious about your faith now. I surely hope you don't let that change, like I did." Nor did he try to make me commit to being a pastor.

Over the years, as people have learned about this deathbed discussion, they have assumed that I became a pastor out of some obligation to please Dad, or because I felt guilty about having abandoned him that summer. Neither of those things is true. I have struggled with pastoral ministry in many ways over the years, but none of those ways has had anything to do with Dad. He loved and treated me with pure grace until the very end.

Dad would live only four more days. In my fear, denial and repression, I spent those days hauling grain for a local farmer.

Dad had been moved to our local hospital, and Mom woke me up in the middle of the night on Thursday to tell me that Dad had died. It was August 12, 1965.

I tried to be strong. I tried to trust my faith. I tried to let my family and friends console me. But I was broken. Totally broken. And lost. Like a good Norwegian boy, I tried to hide my pain.

The next few days are a blur. However, I do remember noon of the day Dad died. The doorbell rang. I trailed Mom as she walked to the door and opened it. There stood Ansel, tears streaming down his face. He didn't say a word; he just held out his hand to Mom.

How strange it was to go with Mom, Neil and Alan to meet with the local funeral director to pick out a casket for Dad and to make the other arrangements that go with a funeral. Mom and Dad had already chosen their plot at the North Viking Cemetery, so we didn't have to make any decisions about that.

We also met with Pastor Elmo to plan the worship service, which would be held on August 16, three days short of Dad's 54th birthday. We all shared ideas as to which hymns we wanted to be sung by the congregation, as well as other parts of the worship service.

People began stopping by the house over the next few days, always something in hand, such as what we call a "hot dish" (casserole) in the Midwest, various salads and desserts: pies, cookies or cakes. Preparing food would not be an issue for several days.

The day of the funeral arrived and I put on the one sport coat I owned, along with a shirt and tie. We gathered in the lounge of the new Sunday School wing with the relatives able to make it to Maddock, and eventually Pastor Elmo joined us for prayer.

Finally it was time for the service. The way our sanctuary was set up for funerals, the family entered the sanctuary from a side door near the right front of the altar area. I had picked our entrance hymn, "My Hope is Built on Nothing Less." We walked into the sanctuary as the congregation sang it. I sang along, but looked down at the floor as we processed in, unable to bring myself to meet the eyes of the congregation. We took our seats in the front pew, turned towards the altar and continued singing.

Now, Maddock was known to be a musical town. Not only did we have good choirs in church and in school, but to this day the community puts on musicals and other special concerts. However, that day the singing of the entrance hymn seemed more powerful than ever. I felt like I was being surrounded with love and lifted into the heavens. Finally, I just had to look back to see this congregation of people singing from their hearts.

To my surprise, there, scattered throughout the congregation, were nearly every member of the Bible camp staff I had been a part of, some forty-strong, in their green corduroy staff jackets, with tears in their eyes, singing with heavenly gusto. I had no idea they were coming to the funeral!

Then I understood, in a way I have never forgotten, what it means to be "surrounded by so great a cloud of witnesses," as Hebrews 12:1 puts it.

Pastor Elmo preached from Romans 8, where Paul proclaims that "I am convinced that neither death, nor life, nor angels, nor rulers, nor things present, nor things to come, nor powers, nor height, nor depth, nor anything else in all creation, will be able to separate us from the love of God in Christ Jesus our Lord."

Bill Raaen had returned to sing Dad's favorite hymn: "How Great Thou Art":

Oh Lord my God,
When I in awesome wonder
Consider all the worlds
Thy hands have made.
I see the stars,
I hear the rolling thunder,
Thy power throughout
The universe displayed.

Then sings my soul,
My Savior, God, to Thee.
How great thou art!
How great thou art!
Then sings my soul,
My Savior, God, to Thee.
How great Thou art!
How great Thou art!

When Christ shall come,
With shout of acclamation,
And take me home,
What joy shall fill my heart!
Then I shall bow
In humble adoration
And then proclaim:
My God, how great Thou art!

When the service was over, we climbed into the funeral coaches for the procession to the cemetery a mile south of Maddock. It was a beautiful, sunny day as we gathered around the casket for the last rites: "In sure and certain hope of the resurrection to eternal life through our Lord Jesus Christ, we commend to almighty God our brother, Edrei Arnold Erickson, and we commit his body to the ground; earth to earth, ashes to ashes, dust to dust. The Lord bless him and keep him. The Lord make his face shine on him and be gracious to him. The Lord look upon him with favor and give him peace."

When death occurs, a combination of shock and adrenaline kicks in and we find meaning, and avoid directly confronting the pain of loss, by focusing on creating the perfect funeral service for our beloved. I have not only experienced this in my losses, but I have witnessed it as a pastor. I have learned to be open to changes in the service to the very end because each family is obsessed with getting it "just right."

In addition, the outpouring of love and compassion moves us greatly. Whether it be the tears in another's eyes, such as Ansel coming to our door, all the folks stopping by the house, the family and friends who gather around us in the funeral service: all of these things feel unbelievably loving and supportive, and it carries us on "wings of an eagle"-- for a time.

However, when the service is over and family and friends have returned home, we are ill prepared for the sense of loss and emptiness that follows. It is then that reality begins to set in, as we say.

I was left with a terrible sense of loss. Never again would I hunt or play golf or throw a ball with Dad. Never again would I hear his stories or hearty laughter. Never again would I be with him. And then the guilt. I tried to fight it off, but it was there. I had run away from Dad, and given up a whole summer I could have been with him. He had loved me so deeply. Could I not have stood by him in his suffering? Like St. Peter hearing the cock crow in the early morning after the crucifixion of Christ, I felt convicted, knowing I had not stood by Dad in the way I wished I had.

There is no way for me to know which aspects of guilt I felt at that time, and what parts of it would come to consciousness over time. But all that guilt and pain was present at some level of my being.

To deal with it, I soon began a ritual I would repeat almost every night. When it became dark, I would go out into our backyard by myself. I would look up at the stars, the galaxies, the moon, the planets. I would try to feel Dad's presence in the universe. I would pray to God for forgiveness and healing. Sometimes I cried. Sometimes I felt hollow and emotionless.

I felt deeply what Anne Lamott writes: "When I die, the people to whom I am closest should grieve forever. They should never quite get over me. Otherwise I will seem dead to them, no matter how close I may secretly be." [1]

I hungered to feel close to Dad, and I felt his presence most strongly on those nights looking up at the stars, the heavens. In spite of the grief and guilt, I also felt such a strong sense of gratitude for having had a father like him. Then, and to this day, I can say to him: "Thanks for not only sharing your faith with me, but even more so, for the unconditional grace and love I always felt from you. I don't know how you did it, but there has never been a moment in my life when I did not feel loved by you."

---

[1] Anne Lamott, Stitches: A Handbook on Meaning, Hope and Repair (New York: Riverhead Books, 2013), p. 40.

Chapter 2   Mom

Lady of silences
Calm and distressed
Torn and most whole
Rose of memory
Rose of forgetfulness
Exhausted and life-giving
Worried reposeful
The single Rose
Is now the Garden.
—**T. S. Elliot**

You are looking for your mother. You keep sitting at the
kitchen table, hoping she will appear.
—**Gail Roen Pearson**

"Brian, why do you sing such sad songs?" Mom was
standing in the doorway to my bedroom. I was sitting on my
bed, playing guitar and singing. It could have been one of the
many songs I loved to play and sing, especially those in minor
keys. I loved the haunting, sad chords. Especially D Minor and
E Minor.

But this time I was singing a song that I had written
myself on March 13,1966. It was titled "The Lonely Negro,"
and was no doubt inspired by another song I was singing at
the time: "Old Man River." The lyrics went:

I'm not wanted, 'Round this place. Seems that
people,
Hate my race.
I have nothin' to call my own. Not ev'n a friend,
When I'm alone.
Still I hope, wherever I go, Somewhere there's a

place,
For a Lonely Negro.

I'm lonely, I'm scared. Best be movin', God knows
where.
It has always been this way; Prob'bly will be, "Till my
dying day.
Still I hope, wherever I go. Somewhere there's a
place,
For a Lonely Negro.

Loss leads to grief, which in turn leads to sadness. Sadness is to grief what shame is to guilt. Guilt occurs when we have done something wrong and we know it. I felt guilty because I had abandoned my dad as he was dying.

Shame is more generalized. You sense you are deficient in some way, but you don't really know what it is. Thus, you don't know how to combat it.

Grief relates directly to a loss and we know what the loss is. Like guilt, it can be extremely intense. Sadness, like shame, is more of a generalized state of being. In a sense, it is like one's whole world has been lost: one's way of life, one's goals, one's purpose, one's sense of how you fit into the universe.

It is not surprising that we find our deepest meaning and purpose in large part through our relationships with those we love most, and through their support of us. When they are ripped away, we flounder, like a fish thrown onto dry land. I sensed that immediately.

In grief time seems to stand still. We are stuck, not knowing how to proceed forward. However, life and chronological time do not allow us to simply push a "pause" button.

Dad died just as summer football practice was beginning: the dreaded two-a-days in the August heat. First, practice at 7 am. Then again at 6 pm, when the farm work for the day was completed. Our pads and practice shirts would not even dry out between practices, so the day began and ended with putting on wet, stinking gear.

Because I am barrel-chested, everyone assumed football must be my favorite sport. Granted, by my senior year, I was 5"11 and weighed 200 pounds, which is a good size for North Dakota Class B football.

However, football was actually my least favorite sport-- one I might well have quit if not for good, old peer and coach pressure (which is stronger the smaller the town.)

From my dad I inherited relatively good eye-hand coordination. This helped me shoot a basketball, swing a baseball bat and pitch, swing a golf club (with putting as my greatest strength), and play tennis, racquetball and table tennis. In football it helped me catch passes, and that is why I was a tight end on offense.

However, I was slower than a combine on a farm road, and my vertical jump was about four inches. Alas, my football coach once said I had the slowest feet and the fastest hands in football. I can't remember dropping many passes, but I was so slow I was rarely open for a pass.

However, the real reason I didn't care much for football is because, at heart, I am a non-violent person, and I don't care what anyone says, football is, in essence, a violent sport. Nearly every play has to do with hitting someone as hard as you can or avoiding being hit. Okay, I admit that, once in awhile, when playing defensive end, and I had a chance to "sack" the opposing quarterback, my juices got flowing. But it was pretty much wasted juice, because I seldom could catch the speedy and sneaky quarterbacks.

However, on the whole, I didn't like the idea of hurting anyone and I wasn't especially excited about getting hurt myself. The most common football injuries are to the neck, knees and ankles, all of which can ruin a basketball, baseball or golfing career.

My foray into violence ended one day in the school playground, some time after having pushed that kid to the ground. The same buddy, Billy (who had been a part of that episode) and I got into a fight about who knows what. I decided to try out what I had seen on TV westerns. I put my right hand into a fist and threw a right hook at Billy's face, squarely meeting his jaw.

I don't remember what happened to poor Billy, but that night my hand hurt like crazy. I thought it might be broken. I couldn't shoot a basketball or throw a baseball. I was scared. I knew I should get an X-ray, but I surely wasn't going to tell Mom or Dad what had happened, and, even worse, Billy's dad was the only doctor in town.

I tried to cover my pain, hope that healing would occur naturally, and I decided never to try to hurt someone else again. I think I must have learned my lesson, because I have never been in a physical fight since, except for the time in college when my girlfriend's former boyfriend showed up at her apartment and started punching me. I simply bowed my head, covered by head with my hands, and waited for my girlfriend and her roommate to pull him off. Mahatma Gandhi would have been proud of me.

It was now time to start football practice, but Dad's death and funeral had left me exhausted, without any spirit, emotion or energy. I certainly was not in the mood for two-a-day football practices, and the violent hits involved.

I talked to Mom about this, and she said I needed to talk to Coach Rutten in person. I went down to the school and told him that I had decided I wasn't going to play football anymore, and explained my reasons why.

He listened carefully, and then responded. "We don't have anyone else to kick off or do the punting. Why don't you come to practice, work on those two elements and that is the only thing I will ask you to do in our games."

That was an offer hard to refuse. I wouldn't have to hurt anyone, I likely wouldn't get hurt myself and I could at least be around my buddies, without having to put on cold, wet, stinky clothes.

Looking back, I now realize that Coach Rutten sensed both what I was not able to do at that time, but also what I needed. In fact, I would not be sidelined for long. At half time of our first football game, I ran up to Mr. Rutten and said, "Put me in, Coach."

As is typical of grief, getting back into one's routines helps us to begin to navigate our new and in many ways, painful new reality.

I was not the only person in my family who was sad and dispirited. So was Mom, although I didn't see that clearly at the time.

Whenever we reflect on the past, we project our presents feelings and ideas and questions onto that past. And there is really no sure way to separate those things from what was actually going on inside of us at the time. I don't remember clearly exactly what questions I had as a fifteen-year-old. What emotions. What I observed in Mom.

I call this layering: the questions and insights that pile up over the years. At 15 I had limited questions to ask Mom about how she was doing because I was limited in my ability to sense what her life was really like. As I grew older new insights would come to me, and with them more questions.

For example, when I was about 25 I was having a routine physical with a doctor in St. Paul, and she, of course, asked about my parents. When I told her my dad had died of cancer, she asked what type, and I said I didn't know but described how it started as a growth on the side of his neck. "Oh," she replied, "he smoked!" I replied, "Well, yes," to which she retorted, "So he got cancer from smoking!"

A light bulb went off. This may sound hard to believe, but I had never made that connection. That in turned raised other questions. I wanted to ask Dad what he knew about cigarettes growing up, when he had begun smoking, if it was considered cool when he was growing up to smoke, if he realized the dangers of smoking, or whether the stresses in his life were such that he ignored the dangers, or if he felt addicted.

And so, as the years go by, the insights increase and with them the questions we would like to have asked our loved ones. However, it is often very difficult to go back and correctly unpeel the layering. What is crucial is that we learn how to live in grace, and not torment ourselves because we did not ask certain questions when we had the chance, either out of fear or, more likely, because at that particular time the questions had never occurred to us.

It's funny. I knew my dad was either trying to quit smoking, or Mom had said he could not smoke in the house, because I remember him going out to smoke in the garage in the summer and in the basement in the winter. When I would see him going out for a smoke, I would often join him to chat. It never occurred to me as a 10 year old to ask Dad if he knew smoking was dangerous to his health.

And so I was likely too busy trying to figure out how to move ahead myself to put much energy into what was going on for Mom, Neil or Alan. Neil had returned to Hawaii for work and thus I didn't see what was going on for him. Alan is quite reserved, and I don't remember him talking much about how he felt. And Mom, dear Mom, was trying so hard to be strong for the rest of us.

It wouldn't be until about a year later, in the fall of my junior year, that I would walk toward the kitchen, arrive at the doorway, see Mom ironing clothes with tears streaming down her face, and finally begin to realize how great her loss was. I asked her what was wrong, and all she said was, "Oh, it's nothing." I, of course, knew that wasn't true, but it was clear she did not want to talk about it.

Ruth Lois Brown was a wonderful woman and mother. She was born in Ellendale, North Dakota, on December 29, 1917, while Grandpa Brown was a pastor there. She was the ninth of twelve children, two of whom died as children.

I adored my mom. She was strikingly beautiful, as her family liked to point out. She was warm, loving, quiet and gentle. Many times as a child, when I was bored or sad, I would lie down on the couch, put my head in her lap and she would gently stroke my face and hair.

At other times I would go into the kitchen to find her, tell her I was hungry or bored and she would put me to work. I think Mom must have spent 75% of her waking life in the kitchen area, which was U shaped and decorated in stereotypic 1950's fashion. The cupboards were metal with red counter tops.

We hardly ever went out to eat. Mom did the shopping and always had home-cooked meals waiting for us, three times a day. Supper was served promptly at six p.m. As in many small towns, the fire whistle was blown at noon and six pm, which was the signal it was time to eat. No matter where I was playing, when the whistle blew it was time to run home, wash my hands and take a seat at the dinner table.

Mom, true to her Methodist upbringing, believed in what we called "clean living." As far as I know, she never smoked a cigarette or drank any alcohol. There was, in fact, not a drop of alcohol in our home, although I know Dad enjoyed a beer or two at the golf club, and perhaps something a bit stronger at the Haukness cabin at Detroit Lakes, Minnesota on their annual golf trip.

Mom was long-suffering. She "went without" so we could have whatever we needed. She was the last to take food at the table after Dad and we three brothers had loaded up our plates. She made sure we had clothes before she spent money on clothes for herself. In fact, she sewed most of her own dresses, which is all she ever wore.

Mom was very pious and religious. Every morning she began the day reading the Christ in our Home daily devotional booklet published by the American Lutheran Church. She always attended worship, taught Sunday School and went to her monthly women's Bible study gathering.

She cooked and served food at funerals and weddings and other special events in the life of the congregation. Whenever I had a Bible or religious question, she was the one I went to

Mom was also involved in community clubs, but even more important than all of these were theinformal relationships she had with several women in our neighborhood. Seven of her friends lived

within two blocks of our house. There was a nearly constant buzzing back and forth to have coffee and desserts. Sometimes there were just two of them, sometimes a group of them.

These women were Mom's strength, I am sure, after Dad died. I have no idea, in that reserved, Scandinavian culture how much she felt open to talking about her feelings or in what ways her friends might have encouraged her to talk about them. Support in that context tended to mean just being available to each other, bringing over a dessert to have with coffee or working on a joint church or community project together.

As a sixteen year old I had no way to see how sad Mom was inside or how lonely she felt; that is, not until a year after Dad had died and I caught her ironing clothes with tears streaming down her cheeks.

Some of her struggle was practical. Dad paid all the bills, took care of the car and dealt with things like insurance. Now she had to learn how to do all of that, along with the nearly constant work of cooking and cleaning and sewing and ironing and mending and driving and shopping and caring for two growing, active boys.

Mom also felt she had to be our great protector. These were still the years of the Cold War in which people worried about a nuclear confrontation with the Soviet Union that could lead to the destruction of the planet. This was the era when people were supposed to know where the nearest "fallout shelter" was, in case of war. These were the years when we had regular safety drills at school. The alarm would go off and we were instructed to crawl underneath our desks.

We had a little room for storing canned and pickled goods in our unfinished basement. One day Mom brought Alan and me down to the basement to show us the "fallout shelter" she had created. In addition to the canned food, there was lots of water, a Bible, and devotional books. The tiny room had one of those glass block windows, only about two feet tall, at the top of the room. Mom had nailed a thin piece of pressed wood loosely over the window. I tried hard not to laugh as I asked her, "Mom, do you know anything about nuclear radiation?"

There was also the big issue of what we used to call "making ends meet." My mom had gone to one year of college, at Jamestown College in Jamestown, North Dakota. It was during the Depression, however, and my best guess is she quit because of a lack of funds. Even though she was there only one year (1934-1935), she made a significant impression, as can be garnered from the large number of well wishes written in her school annual:

> Dear Ruthie, Here's to one of the very sweetest girls on the campus. Anita

> Dear Ruth, We had an argument one day about who was the best looking girl in the freshman class and, believe me, you had plenty of support. See you next year. Frank

> Dear Ruth, Keep smiling; it brightens up this world. Madeline

During our growing up she didn't work outside the home, until she took a part time job in the high school office the last three years of Dad's life.

When Dad died I doubt that our family had any savings to speak of or life insurance. That meant the only income would be Social Security, and so Mom needed to find a full-time job in Maddock if we were going to be able to remain there. She was offered a full time position as the secretary in the high school office, as she had already demonstrated that she did very good work. One of the students who worked with Mom wrote me a note over a decade ago, describing her: "I can still remember her soft, gentle ways, and how beautiful she always looked in her pastel pinks and lavenders and grays! Such a striking lady—graceful, inside and out!"

This job was a lifesaver for our family and so, while we had to watch our pennies, we were able to scrape by. In fact, I never noticed a difference in our lifestyle before and after Dad's death. We always had food to eat, clothes to wear (the basics only), dentist and health care, and whatever costs there were for our education. We had money to go to the swimming pool, buy a hunting license and maintain a membership at the Maddock Country Club, which cost $15 a year.

Looking back on that day I found Mom crying, I wonder what her main struggles were? Was she just overwhelmed by life, now having to do everything to raise us boys, manage the money, take care of the home and work outside of it? Or was she mostly lonely, missing Dad so deeply?

I never went to the cemetery to visit Dad's grave, but Mom did. That is where she went to reflect on life and to talk with him about how her day had gone. Looking back, I think her tears were mainly a reflection of her broken heart. As much as she loved us boys, she was struggling to find meaning without the love of her life.

And so the fall of 1965 found us trying to move on without Dad. Mom was working at the school, Alan was an 8th grader in our elementary school and I was a sophomore in high school.

In my grieving my interests began to change and I found myself going to the school library to check out books not required in class, even though I had never enjoyed reading before. In fact, between the end of August and the end of the following May, I read 47 books that were not required in school. Many of them were spiritual books, but they also included classics. I think that, with my world so thrown upside down, I was searching in the classics for perspective, meaning and direction.

I was also exposed to contemporary books that challenged the status quo: Catcher in the Rye, 1984, Lord of the Flies, Franny and Zooey, Animal Farm, Brave New World, and Fahrenheit 451. Other contemporary books dealt with racial injustice: A Raisin in the Sun, The Lilies of the Field, Inherit the Wind, To Kill a Mockingbird, and Freedom Summer,

By now I was getting a lot more involved in our church youth program, called Luther League, not only at the local level, but at the conference, state and even national level. I went to a Luther League conference in the summer of 1966, at which I studied prejudice and racism, such as the outlandish, white supremacist statement that members of the Ku Klux Klan in Illinois had to sign and the repulsive statement in 1932 of the Lutheran Church in Germany that tied faith to nationality. My life-changing involvement with Luther League would lead to my eventual involvement in the struggles of the 1960's, including racism, civil rights, poverty, world hunger and starvation and war.

My world was now beginning to expand beyond Maddock and North Dakota to a better understanding of and interest in these larger issues. And, as often happens in life, those insights also affected my understanding of local issues.

Twenty-six miles from Maddock was the Devils Lake Sioux Nation, then called the Fort Totten Indian Reservation. Fort Totten did not have a high school and so their students were bussed to Maddock to attend high school. There was a dormitory a block from the school where they lived during the week.

My first time on the reservation was in 8th grade when our basketball team went to compete against theirs. During the game, I jumped to block a layup and smashed into the concrete wall the basketball hoop was mounted on. There was no protective mat hanging on the wall and I was left with a broken hand that needed surgery. It was just one sign of how unbelievably poor life looked on the reservation. The houses, cars and schools all looked run down.

At the time I assumed that these folks just did not know how to take care of things. They must have been lazy and undisciplined.

Now, through my opportunities to learn about the structural causes of poverty and racism, I began to see the struggle of my Native American classmates and friends in a new light. That is when the seeds were planted that God might be calling me to be involved in social justice ministry. My involvement in the church would provide many opportunities over the years to exercise that sense of calling.

My sophomore year ended and once again I headed to Red Willow Bible Camp for another summer as a counselor. My friends there were a strong love and support system in my life, especially in my grief journey.

One of the things I still wonder about was what it was like for Mom and Alan during those summers when I was away. Mom had the wonderful support of her many friends, but I know she continued to miss Dad deeply. As for Alan, I don't know what kind of support he felt. Kids his age certainly didn't have the maturity yet to inquire about how he was doing. It is so important in the journey of grief to be surrounded by people who not only support you, but also are available to truly listen when you need to process what is going on in your life. I don't think Alan had that, and I still feel guilty that I had gone my own way and in many ways just left Alan behind. And, even when I was home, I don't think we talked much about Dad.

Looking back I see how relative life is, especially when you are young. This is your first crack at life and you have nothing to compare it to. You just kind of assume this is the way life is. I had two other good friends who had also lost their fathers to death by the time Dad died, so that kind of loss didn't seem completely unnatural to me. There was a part of me that, without really thinking about it, just accepted that this is the way life is. My task, as I saw it, was to just soldier on. I think Alan tried to do the same.

Part of that soldiering on is keeping busy. In fact, it's usually the first thing we do when we experience loss, and we keep doing it as a way to counter grief. The problem with that, however, is that refusing to think about anything in life never makes it better, whether that be growing a garden or learning to live with our pain. It is one of the greatest human myths, and it stymies our growth and our healing. The only good thing I can think of that can come out of this is that it may numb us for a time until we are ready to face the pain head on. But face it we must, at some point, or we will never heal and find hope again.

This is complicated further by the fact that those around us tend to believe the same thing, and they think if they bring up our loss it will make us hurt again. As if we are not hurting when we are alone! Next to one's loving presence, the greatest gift one can give to someone grieving is opportunities to keep talking about what they are going through. Keeping busy never heals grief. It is only healed by walking head on into it and through it, with the support of God and other people. For how long? For as long as we keep encountering the pain, which may go on for years.

But at the time, I had yet to learn this truth. I kept focusing on activities and sports, hoping to find security and meaning again. And so I did not know how to support my mother in her grief, either. Like us boys, she also just soldiered on, strengthened by her deep faith. We seldom talked about Dad. All three of us were busy at school, church and the community.

Our second Christmas without Dad arrived. Mom had a special gift for me. It was the 1966 High School Yearbook, called The Bobcat. It was dedicated to Dad, with this inscription:

> To the memory of one, who as a teacher, principal and friend of the Benson County Agricultural and Training School employed tireless efforts in the field of education and pubic relations.
>
> Who proved himself a true leader in education and civic circles and
> championed the American Way of Life.
>
> A man who helped make this school what it is.
>
> To the memory of Edrei Erickson we humbly dedicate The Bobcat of 1966.
>
> Mom, in her beautiful handwriting, had inscribed: "To

Brian: In remembrance of your Father, Christmas 1966, Mother."

My relationship with Mom was very different from my relationship with Dad. He and I spent so much time together, but we seldom had deep talks about life. Much of our conversations were focused on his teaching me how to play various sports, and then discussing how I did afterwards. Mom and I spent much less time together, but she was the one I went to when I was sorrowful or lonely or when I had questions about church and my faith.

However, there was one great highlight for Mom and me the year after Dad died. Our congregation offered the Bethel Bible Course, which is an extremely intense, comprehensive, in-depth study of the Bible. Mom and I decided to take that course together. We each had our own books, studied hard and went to class together. This led to many great conversations about faith and discipleship.

Winter brought again my favorite sport, basketball. That year I learned a great basketball lesson, and, for that matter, life lesson, in the first game after our Christmas break. We were tied with only a few seconds left. We had the ball. Coach Rutten set up a play whereby I would get the ball along the baseline. The played worked. I got the ball, I shot and made it, the buzzer went off, and the crowd swarmed the floor.

For some reason I just knew that I was going to make the shot. It was then that I learned the power of self-confidence, and thinking positively when you are in the clutch. For the rest of that season, and the next, whenever we needed points at the end of the game, Coach set me up for the last shot. It was a wonderful feeling and experience to have someone you respected place such confidence in you, and also to have the confidence that you could make the final shot, which I did another three times over the next year and a half.

I learned many lessons that year, giving me some joy in the midst of my grief and a new level of self-confidence about what one can do as an individual and as a team to change and improve.

Grief is a funny thing in some ways. It so pervades your life that you think you will never enjoy anything again, but eventually you start to move on and events like making the winning shot fill you with great joy. It surprised me to feel so happy. I started to realize that my life could find meaning again, even without Dad being there to watch my games.

But Mom was still there. Most of the time. Until that winter.

Beginning in the autumn, Mom began to fall ill frequently. We weren't sure what was going on for her, but she stayed in bed a fair amount. Through the winter, her health continued to deteriorate. Eventually we had to take her to the Maddock Hospital. After running a number of tests, the doctor sat down with Alan and me, and I heard for the third time in my life words that I remember exactly as they were said, "Your Mom has cancer."

I was shocked! I was afraid! He had to be kidding! How could this be happening again?

It was so hard to believe that less than two years after Dad's death, we were experiencing this plague again. I tried to be a strong, Christian boy, trusting that somehow this was God's will, as Mom had taught me.

But this time there was a crack in that traditional faith. If you watch children play any kind of game, it will not be long before one of them yells out, "That's not fair." We seem to have this innate sense of justice, at least where it involves our own needs. I kept thinking to myself: "Could this just be a dream? It can't be happening again, can it?"

I was confused and scared. As bad as Dad's death was, it had not completely changed our lives. We still had Mom, we still had our home and we still had our school, community and church families. But what would happen if Mom died?

It was then that a sad word appeared in my consciousness. We would be orphans. We would be parentless.

I also began to feel anger. Anger is something we are taught that we need to control. We can learn how to control the expression of it, but we certainly can't control having it. One of the great difficulties about anger is that we need to direct our anger toward something, but sometimes we can't figure out what that should be.

Should I be angry at God? As a sixteen year old I didn't know that was allowed. I had not yet studied the unbelievable laments of the Bible, which direct their anger at God. My faith was about the only thing keeping me together, so I believed I had better hang on to it as much as I could.

And then a strange thing occurred, something that made me very uncomfortable. I felt anger at Mom. I knew it was totally irrational. You could not find a more loving, gentle, caring mother in the world. But this anger was not about who Mom was. It was about what I, and Alan, needed. We needed Mom to fight for life. We needed her to fight for health. We needed her to conquer this cancer and get our lives back to normal!

Alan and I tried to go about life as usual. That spring our class play was, "A Man Called Peter," about the famous Christian pastor, Peter Marshall. I had the role of Peter. Maybe playing the part of this famous preacher would strengthen my faith.

I visited Mom in the hospital often, but I could see that she was not getting any better, and the doctor was not providing us with much hope for her recovery. In late March he told us they could no longer give her adequate treatment in Maddock, and she needed to be moved to a larger hospital in Fargo.

Mom sent me to our house across the street to get a suitcase so she could pack up the few things she needed to take to Fargo. I quickly grabbed the best suitcase we had and took it over to Mom's room in the hospital. She took one look at it and said, "That's not the suitcase I want." Then she told me to go back home and get the little, black one that she had gotten from her parents, and had used ever since that one year she attended Jamestown College.

My older brother Neil eventually came home from Hawaii in mid-April and rented a hotel room near the hospital. Alan and I continued in school and various friends and neighbors drove us the 200 mile drive each way to Fargo so that we could visit Mom.

The community of Maddock pulled together to support the Erickson boys. Every night we were invited to a different home for dinner. All we had to do was pour a bowel of cereal for breakfast at home, eat lunch at the school cafeteria and then go to someone's home for dinner. I think I put on about fifteen pounds that spring.

I kept track of those meals. Nineteen different families had us over to their homes providing sixty-three separate meals. They also brought over numerous plates of cookies and bars, washed our clothes and a group of women even cleaned our house. At the bottom of the list I wrote: "All I Can Say Is: Praise and Thank God for Real Friends."

In early April Mom wrote Alan and me from the hospital. She wondered if we were still getting invited out to eat every evening, and gave us the names of three of her friends who had volunteered to do our laundry. She told us how much she appreciated our recent visit and informed us that she had finally been moved to a private room, stating how she wished she had had one earlier when we were there so that we could have visited more easily. She ended her letter: "Do take care of yourselves. I love you both dearly. Lovingly, Mother"

It did not take long to learn that Mom was not responding well to treatment. Eventually Neil called us to say Mom was nearing death. The cancer had spread to her liver, and she was becoming seriously jaundiced.

In early May Pastor Elmo took us to Fargo. Mom was so weak by then that we had to wear gowns and masks when we visited to protect her from further germs. I stood off to the side, focused strictly on her. I have no idea what everyone else was talking about, but I noticed she kept trying to raise her arm, which she could barely do, as weak as she was. I could not figure out what she wanted or was trying to say. Finally I noticed that the sun was shining directly into her eyes. I said, "Mom, do you want me to pull the window shade down?" She smiled, and I went ahead and pulled it down.

One of the things I have noticed over my many years of making visits to hospitals is that anxious and fearful family members tend to jabber. Their loved one can be dying right before their eyes, and they will talk about the weather and whether the Twins won the baseball game the night before. That is why I take the family outside of the hospital room and instruct them: go into the room one at a time to talk with your loved one alone. Do two things. Ask for forgiveness for anything that bothers you, and then tell them how much you love them and how much you appreciate their love.

After everyone had a chance to visit with Mom, Pastor Elmo took out his Bible and led us in a devotion and prayer. Then everyone, including me, left the room. As we entered the hallway and everyone began to take off their gowns and masks, I left mine on, told everyone to go on ahead without me, and that I would be along shortly.

Deep inside me I remembered that I had not said goodbye to Dad in the way I had wanted. I was not going to make that mistake again.

I went back into Mom's room and this time went right up to her bed. She looked at me with such love, and the tears began to well up in my eyes. "Mom," I said, "I'm sorry I have to wear this mask because I really want to kiss you. But I want you to know how much I love you and how much I appreciate all the things you have done for me. You have been the most wonderful mother in the world."

I left the room, took off the medical gear, and headed down the hallway alone. I knew I would not see her alive again. I felt like I was walking into a dense fog. I could not see how or when I would come out of it.

A few days later, May 12, 1967, was our high school prom. My date, Margaret Ann Haukness (from across the street) and I went to the high school for the Grand March and formal festivities, and then   returned home to change clothes for the after party, which was a progressive dinner hosted by several classmates.

When I walked into our house Alan was waiting for me. Neil had called to say Mom had died. Margaret Ann was receiving the same news from her parents across the street. When she came out and joined me in our car, she looked at me with tears in her eyes, and said: "Why does everything have to happen to you?"

She had captured in that simple sentence everything that I was feeling. But, of course, I tried to be brave and cheerful. I did not want to ruin the rest of her night or that of my friends. .

The next few days were a blur. Neil, Alan and I went back to the funeral home to pick out a casket for the second time. We met with Pastor Elmo to plan another service for May 17, 1967. We picked the pallbearers, beloved neighbors and friends.

This time our soloist was Pastor Elmo's wife, Norma, who had become very good friends with Mom, and had visited her often as she was dying. Her first solo spoke of:

> Green pastures are before me,
> Which yet I have not seen;
> Bright skies will soon be o'er me,
> Where darkest clouds have been.
> My hope I cannot measure,
> My path to life is free;
> My Savior has my treasure,
> And He will walk with me.
> [In Heavenly Love Abiding]

I tried to be happy for Mom. She wasn't suffering anymore. She was no doubt free as the hymn put it. But I did not feel free. I felt lost. Lost and alone.

Pastor Elmo preached on Hebrews 11, at the suggestion of Alan, who had quoted this passage in a letter he had sent to Mom: "Now faith is the assurance of things hoped for, the conviction of things not seen." [Heb. 11:1;NRSV] Alan even remembered that Pastor Elmo had used a similar passage at Dad's funeral: "We look not at what can be seen but at what cannot be seen; for what can be seen is temporary, but what cannot be seen is eternal." [II Cor. 4:18;

NRSV]

One of the strange things about the spiritual journey is what comforts us and what does not, which often depends on the setting.

In times of sorrow and loss we rightly turn to the great traditions that have sustained believers throughout the centuries. We sing the hymns, pray the prayers and recite the Scriptures that have brought comfort and hope in the past.

It is one thing to do that on a beautiful, sunny, Sunday morning, when all seems right with the world. It is another thing to do that in the midst of grief. I knew I should put my trust in what cannot be seen. I should put my trust and hope in the eternal. But staring at Mom's coffin, I was having trouble doing that. I wanted to feel hope, but I didn't. All I knew and could feel was that I wanted Mom back with me.

Then came the second solo, "O Holy Spirit, Enter In:"

> Left to ourselves, we shall but stray;
> Oh, lead us on the narrow way,
> With wisest counsel guide us
> And give us steadfastness that we
> May ever faithful prove to Thee
> Whatever woes betide us.
> Come, Friend, and mend
> Hearts now broken, Give a token
> Thou art near us,
> Whom we trust to light and cheer us.
>
> Thy heavenly strength sustain our heart
> That we may act the valiant part
> With Thee as our Reliance,
> Be Thou our Refuge and our Shield.

We Lutherans love to distinguish theologically the Law from the Gospel. The Law is the things we are supposed to do. The Gospel is the Good News that God loves us and accepts us just as we are. This hymn struck me not as Gospel, but as Law. Could I keep from "straying?" Could I walk the "narrow way?" Could I be "steadfast" in my faith? Is there any way I could act the "valiant part?"

I was stuck in these thoughts as once again, on a beautiful, sunny, North Dakota day, we climbed in the funeral coaches for the short drive to the cemetery. There was a hole in the ground, right next to Dad. It was covered with that artificial grass, as if that could keep us from reality. And again, the words of the final commitment: "In sure and certain hope of the resurrection to eternal life through our Lord Jesus Christ, we commend to almighty God our sister, Ruth Lois Brown Erickson, and we commit her body to the ground; earth to earth, ashes to ashes, dust to dust. The Lord bless her and keep her. The Lord makes his face shine on her and be gracious to her. The Lord look upon her with favor and give her peace."

Mom may have been at peace, but I was not. A part of the spiritual journey is lethargy, sullenness. But I did not know that when I was sixteen. I thought I had to be "strong in the Lord," but I felt like I was beginning to sink. Sinking into an unknown world that felt strange and scary to me.

Once again we were surrounded by such a great crowd of witnesses. Four families in Maddock offered to take Alan and me into their homes and families: Gavin and Helen Foss, farmers I had worked for; Leonard and Myrtle Wick, the superintendent who had given Mom a full-time job; Pastor Elmo and Norma Anderson; and Ansel and Dorothy Haukness.

It made the most sense to just move across the street with the Haukness family. The others still had kids at home, but Margaret Ann, Ansel's and Dorothy's youngest, was graduating and heading off to college.

We put our house up for sale, and our furniture and belongings were spread out in the front yard for an auction. I could not bear to be there. I could not stand to see strangers taking our things away. I walked across the street and watched from a distance.

Our house was bought by the Swanson family. They allowed us to keep a few things up in the attic: pictures, toys, baseball cards, marbles and a few small memorabilia of Mom and Dad.

Alan and I carried our clothes and a few belongings across the street and moved into the upstairs bedroom where all three Haukness boys had shared a room. I took a bed right across from the window, looking directly at our house. I put a desk there and that became my place to study, always able to look up and see our former home.

I could no longer go into our backyard at night to look at the stars and talk to Dad, and now Mom. I tried the Haukness' backyard, but it wasn't the same. So every night, before I went to bed, I went to the window and looked across the street at our home, and prayed that somehow God would show me a way through my unfathomable grief.

Chapter 3   Thrust from the Womb

We go in different ways to find God, to discover a peace that will help us live, to become ourselves before we no longer have the time to ask the directions.
— 1971 Concordia Cobber Yearbook

Discontent is the first step in the progress of a man or a nation.
— Oscar Wilde

"Close the door! It sounds like Niagara Falls!" Ansel was yelling up the stairs from the Haukness breakfast nook, which was right at the bottom of the stairs.

I had just gotten up and out of bed and was beginning the day as I always did, by "taking a leak," as we used to say. The Haukness kids had never had a bathroom upstairs, but Ansel and Dorothy converted a small child's bedroom into an upstairs bathroom, which was right at the top of the stairs. It was very convenient for Alan and me! But I guess from now on I had better remember to close the door before I relieved myself.

Over the years, when I have been asked to lead a devotion in various church settings, I have often begun with this question: "Where is home for you? And what does it feel like, look like, smell like?" When people have moved around a lot, it is fascinating to hear which place was most like a home to them.

I am eternally grateful that Ansel and Dorothy, and their four children, welcomed us into their home. And they did everything they could to make us feel "at home." But, frankly, it was not the same, and it couldn't be. And that was partly because I wouldn't let it be.

One of the most fascinating things about grief is the loyalties you hold to. I felt loyalty to my dad as my dad, I felt loyalty to my mom as my mom and I felt loyalty to our house as my home. I guess that may be why I could not simply go into the Haukness backyard, look up at the universe and feel close to Dad and Mom in the same way I did in "our own" backyard.

Dorothy and Ansel were very wise and anticipated this dynamic. They made it clear that they would not be operating as our parents. They understood that we had wonderful parents who had already shaped us, and they would just be there to support us as we continued growing up. And they did that very well.

Ansel Andrew Haukness, my Dad's twin by another mother (both were born on August 19, 1911) was born in Boyd, Minnesota, where his father owned a general store. Eventually they moved to North Dakota, first to Fillmore, then Minnewaukan, and finally to Maddock in 1927. Ansel learned the general store business from his dad growing up, went to college at Concordia for two years and then finished at the University of North Dakota, graduating with a BA degree.

He then moved to Chicago to work for the W. T. Grant Stores, returning to Maddock two years later to work with his father, prior to buying the store from him in 1935.

Dorothy Lillian Moen was born in Williams Country in western North Dakota on October 19, 1918. She attended North Dakota State University, earning a degree in Home Economics. Her first teaching job was in Maddock, where she moved in 1938. It was there that Ansel began to court her, and they were married at North Viking Lutheran Church on June 9, 1940.

Ansel and Dorothy were both intellectually curious people, who kept up on current events and liked to discuss what was going on in the world. Ansel began his day reading the Wall Street Journal, not only for the news but because he was a very successful stock investor. Dorothy also read widely and they both kept up on events by watching the evening news.

Dorothy, like Mom, had grown up in the Methodist Church, and was extremely active in our congregation. She loved to study the Bible and theology, and was actually trained to be one of the Bethel Bible Series teachers, the course that Mom and I had taken together. Over the years she and I would have many fascinating discussions about religion and faith, and I was always impressed by how progressive her thinking was.

She also encouraged me in my style of preaching. Even in those early days I never thought preaching should be just another type of Bible study. The task of the preacher is to study the text, find the kernels of truth and then in the sermon work at "interpreting" the way those ancient truths make a difference in the world today. When Dorothy would hear me preach she would often compliment me on my ability to do just that in a meaningful way.

Ansel was also very active in the church, his favorite involvement being singing tenor in the church choir. During my senior year he and I would go to choir practice together, and then return on Sunday mornings to sing the weekly anthem.

All four of the Haukness kids earned college degrees, or more. The three boys graduated from the University of North Dakota, Steven with a law degree, Paul with an engineering degree and Robert with a business administration degree. Margaret Ann graduated from Concordia College in Moorhead, Minnesota with a degree in elementary education. Steven was the same age as my brother Neil, nine years older than me, Paul 7 years older, Robert 5 years older and Margaret Ann, one year older.

Like my dad, Ansel was a great storyteller, and he never tired of telling the same stories over and over again, often much to the chagrin of Dorothy. I eventually became his straight man: "Ansel, remember the time you and Dad went golfing in Park Rapids?" "Ansel, remember when we decided to haul the garbage from the cabin in your old boat?" And off he would go

All in all, I could not have asked for a better living situation. The problem for me, however, was that I still wanted to be living back across the street, and the Haukness house just didn't feel like home to me. I always felt a bit like a guest, not because of the way they treated me, but because of my own need to be loyal to my former life.

I had lost my center. I was off kilter. I tried to act tough, because I didn't want anyone feeling sorry for me. But I felt as if I had been thrown off a boat at sea and found myself on a deserted island. I wasn't sure where I was, who I was and what I should do to feel safe and centered again.

Alan and I had no sooner moved across the street, finished classes and the baseball season and it was off again to Red Willow Bible Camp. This really seemed like the best thing for me. This was my third year as a camp counselor so it felt more like home to me. Most of my good friends were returning and there really was nothing I loved more in life (other than sports) than working at camp. Once again I felt surrounded by love and support, people were praying for me and I was encouraged to try to be "strong in faith," as we put it.

Alan had been hired to be a Counselor in Training, and I was glad he could also experience the kind of love and support that camp offered, especially so soon after Mom's death.

Once again I fell in love a couple of times, played lots of competitive basketball and softball with my buddies and tried to help the campers in my cabin experience a loving and grace-filled relationship with God. My guitar skills kept getting better and by now we had a singing group that would go around to visit churches on Sundays to lead worship, and I even had some opportunities to preach.

At that point my spiritual journey was still mainly a matter of trying to "tough it out." My mom had taught me that whatever happens in life is God's will, and that we should submit to it no matter how painful or difficult. That was also the gist of the theology I heard at camp. But at camp it was somewhat easier to submit to that theology because I had so many loving people supporting and encouraging me.

Things changed, however, when I returned to Maddock for my senior year of high school. I really missed my buddies from camp, although thankfully two of my camp mates were classmates back home. I decided to up the ante, as we say, and establish a rigorous psychological, physical and spiritual discipline as a way to combat my grief and confusion.

I spent my days at school, and then after school I was involved in my favorite thing: sports. Football and hunting in the fall, basketball in the winter and baseball and golf in the spring. After practice I showered, went home and ate, and then headed directly upstairs to my room.

First I got all of my studies out of the way. Then I worked on Luther League business, as I was now President of the synod Luther League. Reading a non-school book followed this. Then I practiced guitar. After this I wrote a letter to one of my friends. Then I did 50 sit-ups and 50 push-ups. Finally, I read my Bible (I read the entire Bible that year) and then got down on my knees by my bed and spent a lengthy time in prayer. I had started a prayer list right after Dad had died, and by now it had grown to over 200 people. Each night I would pray for one person or family on the list, as well as about other things I was concerned about. Finally, I went to the window, looked across the street at our house and crawled into bed.

Throughout that senior year in high school I actually kept a chart of the activities described above. This included letters written and received. During my high school years I received and sent around 650 letters.

I don't think this rigorous process really helped heal my pain that much. But it kept it at bay, making it possible for me to function.

I still found most of my joy in sports and outdoor activities. My neighbor took me duck and goose hunting (I had not hunted waterfowl with Dad) and I remember how thrilled I was when I bagged my first goose. We also had another successful football season, again winning our conference, going undefeated.

The holidays were soon coming, my first ones in the Haukness home. One of the things I enjoyed most living in the Haukness house was the intriguing discussions held in the living room, especially on holidays and special events like school reunions, when a lot of folks were home visiting. Their living room easily held 7 or 8 people in a kind of rectangle, and people loved to stop by to visit. I loved to just sit there as people came and went, joining in the great variety of topics that would be brought up.

I got my first taste of the delightful living room conversations at both Thanksgiving and Christmas of 1967. Not everyone in the family could get home every year, but whoever was there participated in these lively discussions. And by that time those discussions included the Vietnam War, which was continuing to escalate, and creating tremendous dissension in our country, including on college campuses.

The reality of that war hit home between Thanksgiving and Christmas. When I was a freshman, a senior, Norman Williams, and I played side by side in football. He took me under his wing and taught me some of the basics of blocking. But that December, at age 21, he was killed in Vietnam. The news sent shock waves through our little community. It would put a real pale on Christmas as we grieved with Norman's family.

What also hit home was that Steven Haukness was not with us that Christmas. After he graduated with a law degree from the University of North Dakota, he had joined the State Department as a civilian, and had been stationed in Vietnam. It was hard not to worry about him.

A mere month later, in January of 1968, Steven flew north to Hue, the old, imperial Vietnamese capitol, during the Vietnamese holiday Tet, during which a temporary truce was typically called. His friend from the State Department was engaged to a woman from Hue and her family was planning a large dinner to celebrate both the holiday and the upcoming wedding.

He stayed with another friend who was a Foreign Service officer in Hue. After the formal dinner on January 30,

Steven and his friend headed back to this friend's apartment.

In the middle of that night, the Tet Offensive began. Before it ended, Steven would "disappear." His friend's body was found, but not Steven's. We did not know if he had been killed or taken as a prisoner of war. We clung to the hope that he was a prisoner.

We all entered into a painful period of uncertainty, not knowing what to believe or feel. This was especially difficult for Steven's wife, Alpha, and their two young, twin boys. What was she supposed to do with her life now? When would she find out the truth? Would she ever find out the truth?

The weeks turned to months, and then eventually years, and we still heard nothing more about Steven.

Grief comes in so many strange shapes and forms. As difficult as it is, it is one thing to know someone is dead, to then go through the grieving process and begin to eventually rebuild a new life. But what do you do when you don't know if the person is dead or not? You cling to hope, knowing it could be shattered at any moment. You try not to give in to despair, but cannot plan for the future. Our family was left in purgatory, caught between heaven and hell, not knowing whether to nurse hope or grieve a loss.

We all tried, as best we could, to return to our normal activities. I focused on basketball and we had another good year, both as a team and for me individually, again averaging nearly 20 points a game.

It was also time to focus on college, which was an easy decision for me. Many of my friends from camp had been going to Concordia College in Moorhead, Minnesota, a liberal arts school of the Lutheran church. Since I was still thinking of going to seminary eventually, this seemed like a natural fit. However, there was one problem, one that would turn out to be significant.

Mom had left a will, making Neil the legal guardian of Alan and me. He was also put in charge of managing what little estate there was. Mom had left instructions in her will that "Brian and Alan should receive a good education, and then the money will be divided three ways." Neil had gone to Wheaton

College in Chicago for one year and then to the University of North Dakota in Grand Forks, where Alan also planned to go. It was considerably less expensive than Concordia, and this created tension between Neil and me.

There is nothing my parents wanted more than for the three Erickson boys to get along. And, when we were younger, we more or less did. However, my parents' wishes did not take into account the dynamics of what we call in psychology, the "family system."

Our family system was actually fairly classic. Neil was a typical oldest child. He was driven, a high achiever, very disciplined, somewhat rigid, took responsibility and expected loyalty in return, and he served in the military, as a reservist.

I am a fairly typical middle child. I am rebellious (no one can tell me what to do), fun loving, progressive politically, and the great mediator, just wanting everyone to get along.

Normally the youngest is the easy going one who is more of a follower than a leader, who enjoys the present and likes to have a good time, and is faithful to the other family members. Alan certainly played that role, and over the years has been as supportive as any brother could be.

My parent's dream of three loving brothers getting along and relishing each other's company forever began to crack soon after we lost our parents. Neil, filling what he considered to be his fiduciary responsibility, was bothered that I would end up spending more of the inheritance than he thought I should. This was compounded by the fact that I did not heed his advice as my older brother to go to the University of North Dakota or North Dakota State rather than Concordia.

One of the most difficult things about life is that loss and tragedy often are not self-contained. One experience of suffering sometimes leads to, if not causes, another.

One could argue that it was random that my mom should die so shortly after my dad. And yet, as time went on, I became increasingly convinced that she died of a broken heart.

If our parents had lived long lives, perhaps we three brothers would have gotten along just fine. But I believe our inability to talk openly about our loss and grief, and our attempts to repress what was going on inside of us, had a part (perhaps a big part) in the conflicts we would have over the years. The issue of where I would go to school was only the beginning of a long series of painful disagreements.

The summer before college I headed off once again to be a counselor at Bible camp, this time in California. This was a wonderful change and an eye-opening experience. Working just south of the Bay Area near Santa Cruz, we got a real taste of the counter-culture and anti-war movement centered there.

Martin Luther King, Jr., had been assassinated only two months before in Memphis. While we were en route to California, Robert Kennedy was assassinated in Los Angeles. I was confused by these tragic events, and began to realize I needed to learn a lot more about the dynamics of racism and violence in our country.

Soon enough, we were heading back to North Dakota, packing my bags and heading to Concordia. Margaret Ann was already a student there. Ansel and Dorothy drove me to school where we met up with Margaret Ann, who showed me the ropes. I had arranged to live in a dorm with one of my buddies from Bible camp, Steve Carnal. He introduced me to several of his friends (he had already been at school one year) and I settled in for my first year of college.

I was nervous about school. When you come from a small school system like Maddock, you naturally wonder how your educational background compares to that of students from larger cities and school districts. Complicating things further was the fact that I was still struggling psychologically. My world had been thrown upside down, and I was nowhere near having fully adjusted.

I missed Mom and Dad. I wished they were available to give advice and help me make decisions. When I would see students arriving with both of their parents, I felt jealous.

Neil had returned to Hawaii and we hardly ever saw him. He didn't seem particularly interested in what was going on for Alan and me and, as already indicated, I wasn't particularly open to his advice anyway.

My psychological situation was complicated further by the fact that I was beginning to realize I felt angry with Mom. I didn't want to feel that way, but I just couldn't help it. It wasn't as if I thought she wanted to die. But I wondered why she couldn't have been stronger, and fought harder against the cancer. I knew she missed Dad. I knew her heart was broken. But she still had two boys living at home who adored her. Wasn't that enough to give her the will to live?

The more I learned about cancer over the years, the more my anger was reinforced. I witnessed how much the will to live makes a difference in fighting cancer. As a parish pastor I saw people just give in to cancer, and die soon. I saw others fight and fight, and live long after the doctors had said they would. Why hadn't Mom been able to do that? Weren't Alan and I important enough to her to fight for every day of life possible? Such were the questions and feelings percolating within me.

Beginning my college studies, in the midst of so many ambiguous feelings, was difficult. My tuition was covered, but beyond that I didn't have much money, and I had no place to turn when I needed funds. Neil had made it very clear that I was already taking too much

I also wasn't sure, to be frank, about what I wanted to do with my life. Yes, I had been thinking a long time about being a pastor, but I had many concerns about the profession. I had worked with lots of pastors at Bible camp, and I didn't always like what I saw. Many of them were too serious and pious. Many of them put their whole lives into their work, and I had so many other things I wanted to do in life. And, if I ended up in a small town--like Maddock--as most pastors did, at least in the beginning, I wasn't sure I wanted to live where everyone knew who I was and I was expected to be a role model for the entire community. Yes, as I had already experienced, a small town can be wonderfully supportive when you are hurting, but it can also be hard to live in a "fish bowl" where everybody knows what everybody else is doing.

However, as I have learned several times in life, a great

anecdote to confusion and insecurity is falling in love. This happened quickly at Concordia and I had several weeks of being on a "Rocky Mountain high" until Pauline Marie Peterson unceremoniously dropped me like a sack of flour, as described in the Prologue.

This whole episode was not particularly helpful to my self-confidence. I once again turned to sports to soothe my wounds and my broken heart. I was excited to try out for the freshman basketball team. I had gotten myself in good shape and was shooting the ball very well. I knew the only position I could play in college would be guard, as I had done in my younger years, and I also knew my lack of speed was going to be a challenge.

I ended up playing guard a lot with another frosh trying out, Joel Gilbertson, from Williston, North Dakota. We had fun passing to each other, setting screens, running plays, and shooting from the outside. The last practice before making cuts Joel and I were on fire, burning off the nets, and we were quite sure we would both make the team. But when the final roster was posted, our names weren't on it. I was dumbfounded. And then I noticed four football players had made the team, despite not being at the tryouts. Just like when we were kids, we blurted out, "That's not fair." But there was nothing to be done about it!

This was not the blow I needed. All my life sports had been my refuge, and now there would be no practices, no games, no camaraderie. The only good thing that came out of it would be that Joel and I would end up living together the next three years, and we are great friends to this day.

Instead, Luther League became my primary activity, and my main form of church involvement. Bible camp had been important to me in terms of reaffirming the importance of faith in my life, and of giving me a sense of the importance of a loving and supportive community when you are going through difficult times. What Luther League gave me was a chance to see the pain of the world, and what the church might be called to do about that pain and suffering. In mid-October I headed to Omaha, Nebraska for the church's National Convention as part of a youth delegation. Here I was exposed to resolutions and heated debate on the issues of race, poverty, and the war in Vietnam. We heard a report from the Black Lutheran Clergy Group about the issues they saw as important. Resolutions and discussion were held on world hunger, the Vietnam War, the importance of reducing nuclear armaments and the church's support of Selective Conscientious Objection to war.

As I look back on that era, the image that comes to me is that of the aging of a potato. In the 1950's, right after World War II, the church blossomed and grew. People came to church in their Sunday best. We were proud of our country and we believed the United States was the "good guy" in international conflicts. Our country welcomed the world's tired and downtrodden. In most church sanctuaries there was both a Lutheran flag and an U.S. flag, side by side, and that seemed to be entirely appropriate.

The church was like a ripe, fresh potato, pulled from the earth. As a potato ages, it begins to shrink and get wrinkled, and eventually root shoots begin to grow out of it. You can either cut those shoots off, leaving the potato wrinkled and shrinking, or you can nurture those shoots and allow them to fall back into the earth and sprout new life.

I was beginning to sense that the church was, most of the time, at least at the local level, choosing the former. My hope came at the national level where I saw growing attempts to shed destructive views of the past and attempt to become open to the clamors for change coming from the poor and oppressed, both in the U.S. and around the world. I was quickly becoming exposed to a new world that challenged the church's rosy picture of itself and our nation--the proliferation of nuclear weapons, the colonial and immoral aspects of the Vietnam War (including the bombing and killing of thousands of civilians), the lack of civil rights for blacks, Native Americans, Mexican farmworkers and others in our country, the prejudice towards gays and lesbians, and eventually, the secondary way in which women were still being treated.

Right after returning from Omaha, we had our annual Luther League Convention in Fargo. We showed the film "A

Time for Burning" about a white, Lutheran pastor in Omaha trying to persuade his all-white congregation to reach out to a black congregation in the northern part of the city. The film includes a meeting between the white pastor and a black barber, Ernie Chambers, who tells the pastor that his Jesus is "contaminated." The outreach effort is not successful, mainly because of the refusal of white parishioners to reach out to the black church, and the white pastor ends up resigning his call.

At the end of the convention I had put together a presentation on the theme that the church needed to give up some of its traditions if it wanted to be "real" to the needs of modern youth. Although received favorably by many folks, my bishop received complaints that our conventions were not traditional enough, and that my leadership was going in the wrong direction.

Later that month, when third party presidential candidate George Wallace came to Fargo to speak outside the Civic Auditorium, I went to hear him. I still have an actual picture of him speaking taken from behind, and you can see me in the crowd. Compared to what I had been learning through the church and my classes about the civil rights movement, I was appalled by Wallace's racist and white supremacist sentiments.

Because of this growing interest in issues of prejudice and race, in my first semester at Concordia I had managed to get myself into a 200 level religion course, "Seminar on Race Relations." We read James Baldwin's Go Tell It on the Mountain, Claude Brown's Manchild in the Promised Land, Charles Silberman's Crisis in Black and White, Ralph Ellison's Invisible Man, Nathan Wright Jr.'s Black Power and Urban Unrest, Stokely Carmichael's and Charles Hamilton's Black Power: The Politics of Liberation, and Martin Luther King, Jr.'s Stride toward Freedom.

This class had a powerful impact on me, as can be seen in my final paper, which ended with a prayer: "I pray that I may have a part in the great task of reconciliation—reconciliation of white to white, black to white, black to yellow, people to people, and . . . oh, yes . . . in the process, maybe me to You and in a way I never dreamed possible. Dear God, I'm ready. Where do we go from here?"

That Christmas I was again back with the Haukness family. There was a somberness hanging over our Christmas celebration, as we still knew nothing more about what had happened to Steven.

Once again I received the gift of a high school yearbook, the 1968 edition from my senior year. This time it was not from Mom. Instead, it was dedicated to her:

To a person who gave unselfishly of her time in service to
her family, church, school and community;
—who lived her life as an example that all could emulate;
—who, in a quiet way, inspired effective leadership to all;
—who was loved and respected by all who knew her;
We, the student body and faculty of the Benson County
Agricultural and Training School do humbly dedicate
this Yearbook to the Memory of Mrs. Ruth Erickson.

As I read that dedication on Christmas Eve, I felt a strange churning inside me. I still wasn't comfortable at Concordia, but I also knew I was being thrust out of my eighteen years of life in Maddock. There was a kind of finality in reading that dedication to Mom, a finality that really did feel like an ending.

It was time for me to be born into a new life. I had been playing around the edges in terms of challenging my traditional theological views and opening myself up to the great social issues of the day. Now it was time to really leave the womb of the life I had known and open myself up to embrace the new world into which I was being pulled.

In six months the first humans would be thrust through the gravitational pull of the earth in order to land on the moon. I also was being thrust from the world I had known into a new world. I wasn't sure what that world would be like, but I sensed deep within that it was time to take what Kierkegaard, the Danish theologian, calls "the leap of faith," in trust that a new universe awaited me that would breathe life into my weary soul.

Chapter 4   Rebirth

I will tell you what I will do and what I will not do. I will not serve that in which I no longer believe, whether it calls itself my home, my fatherland, or my church: and I will try to express myself in some mode of life or art as freely as I can and as wholly as I can, using for my defense the only arms I allow myself to use -- silence, exile, and cunning.
-- **James Joyce, "A Portrait of the Artist as a Young Man"**

When life itself seems lunatic, who knows where madness lies? Perhaps to be too practical is madness. To surrender dreams — this may be madness. Too much sanity may be madness — and maddest of all: to see life as it is, and not as it should be!
— **Miguel de Cervantes Saavedra, "Don Quixote"**

Jesus answered him, '"Very truly, I tell you, no one can see the kingdom of God without being born from above." **-- John 3:3 (NRSV)**

    "So what are you reading and thinking about now?" Christmas was over. As I prepared to head back to school, I had dropped by to see Pastor Elmo.
    I shared that I was now pretty sure I no longer wanted to major in psychology, as originally planned, and that I was thinking about trying some courses in philosophy to see where that might lead. I explained that I wasn't ready to delve further into Christianity right now, but needed to take a more objective, analytic approach to the search for meaning, which philosophy would offer.
    "Well," Pastor Elmo continued, "whenever you are home be sure to stop by so we can discuss what you are reading and thinking about." Little did he know that this was an offer that would lead to hours upon hours of discussions whenever I

was home in Maddock, or later, after the fall of 1971, when he would leave Maddock and take a call in Fargo, just across the river from Concordia.

I now had several requirements out of the way and could begin taking more classes in my areas of interest. I had entered Concordia planning to major in psychology. However, the approach at that time was very behavioral oriented, and I realized I am not really a scientist who enjoys watching mice run through a maze or studying the chemistry of the brain.

My big break came when I learned that for my basic requirements I could take a philosophy course rather than mathematics. I didn't know much about philosophy, but I thought I might as well give it a shot as I had already studied a lot of math in high school and was ready to move on from that.

Philosophy is a lot like theology in that it asks the age-old questions about the meaning and purpose of life. However, it does so in a more rational, detached, objective way, which I found to be extremely refreshing.

I eventually majored in philosophy, with a second major in religion, focusing on world religions rather than just Christianity. Within Christianity, my main focus was on ethics, having to do not so much with what one believes as with how one acts.

College was beginning to become what it is supposed to be: a unique opportunity to give concentrated study and attention to the academic aspects of what one wants to focus on in life. The more I got into these subjects, the more I got to know students and professors, the more my self-confidence grew. As I began to feel part of the campus community, I was able to put lost loves and lost sports behind me and move into my future, whatever it was going to be.

However, without being fully aware of it at the time, my studies were also giving me the opportunity to begin to take on theological assumptions that had slowly sapped the energy and excitement from my life.

Like Jacob wrestling with the angel, I grabbed on to God and cried out, "I will not let you go until you bless me." So all my suffering is your will? Either tell me this isn't true, or tell me why you put me through this!

I searched the great theologians and philosophers of the world, pressing them for insights into what I consider to be one of the greatest questions humans face: what is the relationship of our suffering to God's will?

I felt like I was being freed of the traditional shackles that had bound me! I would not go on living this way, because this was no way to live. Was I afraid? Yes! Was I determined? Yes! Sometimes you have to hit bottom before you are willing to take whatever risks are involved in the quest for freedom and healing. It is scary to begin letting go of all you have been clinging to, all that seems to keep you hanging together. But sometimes you just have to let go and let everything come crashing to the ground, and then begin to rebuild from the ground up.

I didn't realize that is what I was doing at the time, but that was no doubt a good thing! I would have been even more scared! Eventually, however, something was going to have to give!

As a college freshman I was required to take a basic Bible course. Looking back, much of what we studied was new to me and has been extremely helpful over the years. We studied the Bible using critical analysis: trying to understand the sources it came from, the form in which a particular text was written, the problems of translation and the author's purpose in writing the particular book. However, although I found less and less satisfaction in blindly trusting traditional doctrine, I also wasn't moved by the objective study of the Scriptures. I hungered for something different.

I found what I was seeking in two places. The first was the amazing, challenging and delightful world philosophy opened up for me. It was relentless in asking the difficult questions about life, and was ripe with all kinds of different responses. What is real? What is ideal? What makes truth? What does it mean to be human? Where do we find meaning in the universe? What is the proper basis of morality? How can we use logic to get at truth, and falsehood?

The second place was world religions. I had grown up

being taught, of course, that Christianity was the only true religion, even taking a course in Sunday School that tried to explain why Christianity was true and other religions were not. Now I had a chance to read for myself the original sources of Islam, Judaism, Buddhism, Hinduism, Zen Buddhism, Taoism and Confucianism. As one might expect, so much of what I had been taught was oversimplification and caricature.

I was especially intrigued by eastern mysticism as found in Zen Buddhism, Taoism and Hinduism. In these religions all of reality is seen as one. God is inherent in that reality, or even, according to Hinduism, the sum total of reality. God is not an outside force working on the world, but is in the world, and we experience God by immersing ourselves in reality. It is inherently naturalistic, celebrating the interconnectedness of nature and all forms of life. God is not found in a cathedral or a sanctuary or worship liturgy, but in creation and the interconnectedness of people.

For a time I put the study of Christian doctrine on the back burner, and, in terms of church, I focused on ethics and social ministry.

As the first school year ended, a wonderful opportunity presented itself. Concordia offered a program called May Seminars, which were intensive, one-month courses around the world.

That year Concordia had chartered an Air France flight for those seminars, but had more seats than students. Concordia students were invited to take advantage of the plane ride for $250 without signing up for a class. You flew to Paris on May 4 and all you had to do was show up for the return flight out of Paris on June 3.

This is one of those things in life that I suspect my parents would not have allowed me to do. For that matter, I don't know if I would want my own kids to do it. However, it was a powerful, experiential way to meet people from other countries and cultures, and to be able to compare what I believed about religion, politics, economics and culture in a more global context.

I made plans with a friend to hitchhike around Europe.

Starting in Paris, we would go to Calais, France, take a ferry to Dover, England, spend several days in London, then hitchhike up to Newcastle and take a ferry to Bergen, Norway. From there we would head to Oslo, Stockholm, Copenhagen, and finally Amsterdam on the way back to Paris.

We boarded that Air France charter in Fargo, all 165 of us, and headed with glee across the pond. I kept a journal throughout the trip, writing about the fascinating places we went and the people we met.

Rick and I knew no French. When we arrived, all we knew was that we were to accompany the rest of the independent travelers to a youth hostel, and then get orientated as to what to do next. From the airport we headed to the subway as a group to travel to the hostel. I wrote in my journal: "Rick and I, being two gentlemen, let everybody else go first—only for the two of us to get blocked off by the gate, separated from the rest of the group."

Watching the train speed off, leaving us behind, we had no idea what to do next. We decided to hop on the next train, and as we came to each stop we looked to see if our group might we waiting for us on the platform where they had gotten off. No dice! And so we kept going until we were on the edge of the city.

Somehow we managed to get off the train and figure out how to cross over the tracks and take the train back into the heart of the city, all the while lugging our backpacks, which were laden with a month's worth of clothes and toiletries.

We found a gas station, but no one spoke English. Then we went to a bar, where we found a man who spoke French and German. At that time I was quite fluent in German, and we managed through him to get something to eat and we convinced the bartender to accept our America dollars.

Twice we tried to call the American embassy, but both times someone who spoke French answered. Go figure! Eventually we were able to find a bank to change our money and secure a cheap hotel, where we ended up crashing at 4:30 pm, exhausted from our overnight flight and the ensuing craziness.

After 19 hours of sleep, we got up to take on the world again. After a hot dog and a beer, we stopped by a French cathedral where we finally ran into some of our group, who showed us how to find our hostel. Reunited at last!

That night we hung out with guys from Italy, Portugal, Algeria and England. With my German and the various languages the others spoke, all of us were able to communicate one way or another. I still remember someone would tell a joke, then it would be translated and someone else would laugh, and then it would be translated again, and another person would laugh, right down the line. This was the beginning of a marvelous adventure and profound learning experience as over the next month we would meet and talk to so many young people, and a few older ones as well, from all around the world.

I also learned soon the disfavor with which Americans are held in many parts of the world for our pompous attitudes and intervention in so many of the affairs of the world, including--especially at that time-- Vietnam.

When we were ready to head to England, Rick and I took the Metro to the outskirts of Paris to catch a ride to Calais. I wrote in my journal, "We waited four hours with no luck. In order to get a ride we either need a female to hitchhike with us or to not be American. Got pretty hacked off." Eventually, we gave in and bought train tickets. It was not a good start on my meager budget.

Hitchhiking was much better once we were in Great Britain, and our adventure continued. One evening Rick and I went into a pub that was swarming with people. We secured the last free table. I noticed a black man standing in the doorway, looking for a place to sit. Since we had two empty seats at our table, I waved him over. Soon we were joined by a friend of his, Charles, from Ceylon (now Sri Lanka), an island nation 20 miles off the coast of India. These two men bought all of our drinks and then Charles invited us to the restaurant he owned for a late dinner. There, at 12:30 am, I was served the finest chicken curry I have ever tasted, along with some of the world's finest wine.

The next day, while writing postcards in a restaurant, a young woman from Madison, Wisconsin, named Pat, approached me and asked if I was American. She ended up spending the day with Rick and me, and eventually, since she was all alone, asked if she could join us hitchhiking.

We left London on our way to Newcastle. Most people did not have room for three hitchhikers, so one of us would go with Pat and the other would go alone. Whoever was with Pat got wherever we were going much sooner.

By the time we reached Oslo Pat and Rick decided to go skiing in Austria. Since I had never skied, and didn't have the budget to add another leg to the trip, we parted ways.

I had a terrible time finding rides in Sweden. In fact, on my first night alone I got stuck out in the middle of nowhere as the sun set. I noticed a small camper trailer out in the woods, and somehow managed to get in. It is always fun to take out your contacts lenses and preserve them in saliva!

The next morning I walked to the nearest town and bought another train ticket, this time to Denmark, where everyone was extremely friendly. I met one man on a ferry between the islands of Denmark who actually took me to his home for dinner, gave me a bed to sleep in and then a ride to the main highway in the morning. It was at that point that luck struck. Standing at the Denmark/German border, a Lamborghini went flying by, the driver pounded his breaks to a stop, backed up, and asked: "Where are you going?" "Amsterdam," I said. "Hop in! That's where I am headed!"

What a ride! I almost wished the Autobahn had a speed limit! All I could do was sit back, try to relax and cast my fate to the wind.

By the time we reached Amsterdam, I had run out of money. Having to buy so many train tickets had thrown my budget entirely out of whack. I immediately went to a Western Union office and wired Ansel for a few dollars. When the money finally arrived, I bought a train ticket to return to Paris.

Soon after I got stateside, my brother Neil came home for a lengthy visit. He was both fascinated and appalled by my trip to Europe, but enjoyed hearing about all of my adventures.

Since his job with GAO (the Government Accounting Office) included travel all over the Far East, he could understand my wanderlust.

That fall I returned to Concordia and moved into Brown Hall with my basketball buddy, Joel, and Stu, a friend of his from Montana. Both would be my roommates my last three years at Concordia.

One evening late in September we were all sitting around our room and Stu and Joel were trying to convince me to get back into the dating game. After Pauline had dropped me with a thud I had had a few dates, but had mainly gone to parties and hung out in male and female friend groups. Joel and Stu challenged me to dial a random four-digit extension to see who on campus might answer. If it was a female, my task was to convince her to go out on a date with me.

So I dialed four numbers and a young woman with a lovely, kind voice answered the phone. I think I said something about dialing a wrong number, but I started to chat with her. I found out she was a frosh and her name was Laura. (All of the names of my girlfriends have been changed out of respect for the survivors, as the Coen brothers say in their Fargo television series). Eventually I asked her to have coffee, and she agreed. Wager won!

Stu and Joel couldn't believe it. We grabbed a copy of Who's Who on campus, and found Laura's picture. I just about dropped dead because she was drop-dead gorgeous.

Believe it or not, Laura would soon become my first real love. I was totally smitten, and she didn't seem to be far behind. We got together often, especially on weekends, but also during the week to drink coffee or study together. We went for long walks in the woods. I read poetry to her, sent her cards, and even wrote her letters, usually filled with poetry. Weekends found us at concerts, movies or parties with friends.

The one thing I was concerned about was an issue that is a common challenge in college. Laura had a boyfriend back home, and she admitted that to me. I wondered, then, if I was just an object for her to have a little fun with at college, or whether I stood a chance compared to the guy back home.

That fall was filled with significant opportunities to keep learning about and promoting social justice issues, including rising awareness of the gay rights and anti-war movements. I also ran for and was elected to the Student Senate.

In my role as President of Luther League for the eastern half of North Dakota, I helped plan our annual convention, which we scheduled for Bismarck as a joint effort with the western part of the state. Our theme was "People Are Dying: And We Say We Care!" As we began to make plans, we realized it is easy to "say" we care. Anybody can pass a resolution suggesting action, but that does not mean anything is going to get done. We came up with a unique idea, one that is still bearing fruit to this day.

Working with CROP (The Church Rural Overseas Program) of the National Council of Churches, we planned the first, ever CROP Walk. During one afternoon of the convention participants walked 10 miles and we raised $16,000, and Laura and I had the opportunity to deliver the check in person to CROP headquarters in Elkhart, Indiana.

I also became involved in the anti-war movement on campus. One fall morning we loaded a school bus in Moorhead to capacity, including Laura and me, and drove the 200 miles to the state capitol in Bismarck. There we marched through the city protesting the war, ending up at the steps of the capitol building, where we read the names of all North Dakota soldiers killed in the war--including my football teammate, Norman Williams--placing their names in a cardboard casket sitting on the top of the steps.

Then came what I still think of as one of the most surreal experiences of my life. The Selective Service System had decided to replace the "draft" with a "draft lottery," which would determine the order of the draft into military service for men born between 1944 and 1950. I wasn't as worried about the draft as most of my friends, because attending seminary would give me a deferment. However, if I decided not to attend, then I would be subject to being drafted like everyone else.

On December 1, 1969, a number of us gathered in a friend's basement apartment with a couple of cases of beer to watch TV. However, this was not Monday Night Football. We were watching 366 blue capsules be drawn out of a tank to see in what order we would be drafted. It felt as though we were watching to see who would live and who would die.

Joel got a low number, 80, which meant there was a good chance he would be drafted. I got a high number, 333, which meant that I would not be drafted, whether I went to seminary or not. I still remember how uncomfortable I felt with that high number when so many others at the party got low numbers. Joel ended up joining the National Guard as a reservist prior to being drafted.

I went to Maddock for Christmas, and afterwards headed to Laura's home in Minnesota. New Years came, I kissed Laura, we left the 1960's behind, and we were ushered into a new decade. Little did I know what the first year of that new decade would hold for me. I entered it thinking I was beginning to find my stride. I felt ready to take on the world. And, in a way I did.

But the world also took me on in ways that would challenge me at the deepest levels of who I am. At the risk of sounding melodramatic, 1970 would become the year that began my spiritual rebirth, although, in the eyes of some, including my brother Neil, it would be the year in which I would go down in infamy.

Early in that year, Laura and I parted ways and my heart was truly broken for the first time. I had thought we were meant to be. My spiritual director liked to say, "You can't know God's will ahead of time." We often think a certain path forward is God's will. Well, sometimes it is, but sometimes it isn't. I had been quite sure Laura and I were "meant" to be together, whatever the spiritual connotations I may have layered on it at the time, but I was, as they say, "sadly mistaken" and "rudely awakened." And it hurt. It really hurt.

One more loss. Another kind of loss. A new kind of loss. The loss of my first love. As a way of repressing my pain and grief, I quickly did what I almost always did: try to find a rebound route. I started dating another woman, wondering if I would ever find anyone I would love as much as I loved Laura.

It seems to me that most of us have lost a "first love" somewhere along the way. We assume that we will never love that way again, and that we will have to settle for something less than our deepest dreams. It's like a friend of mine likes to say, "Some people don't get nice things." He says it whenever the Minnesota Vikings lose in the last few seconds of a football game, which happens more than you could ever imagine.

As my sophomore year ended, an event occurred that sent waves of outrage and grief throughout our campus. At Kent State University on May 4, 1970, the National Guard opened fire on a group of students protesting the Vietnam War, killing 4 and injuring 9, one of whom was paralyzed for life.

Meanwhile, I was about to make one of the biggest mistakes of my life. Throughout that spring Neil and I had been discussing the possibility of my living with him that summer in Hawaii while I took courses at the University of Hawaii.

I don't know exactly why I proposed this idea. I would like to think it was because I thought this would be a wonderful opportunity to get to know Neil better. I think it did include that. But it probably was also a way to live in an exotic place for free, while also getting two philosophy courses under my belt.

I had a great summer, but Neil didn't. I loved my classes, bought a surfboard and spent lots of time at the beach. So what was the problem with Neil? Well, it ranged from my personal behavior to my views on the world.

Neil did not drink alcohol or smoke. Nor did I, until college. You would be hard pressed to find a fellow who grew up in rural North Dakota who did not drink beer in high school. But I was one of them. In a way I was a "goody two shoes" who was trying to live a puritan lifestyle as an outgrowth of my conservative Christian faith.

That quickly changed once I hit Concordia. My friends introduced me to parties and beer and I found it to be a lot of fun. I had no conscious awareness of this at the time, but from the moment I began college, and especially after I didn't make the basketball team, almost every aspect of my life went into rebellion. This was not the typical college type of rebellion, where a student is suddenly not under the nose of their parents and they decide to sow a few wild oats. My parents were gone, the Hauknesses were not trying to control me and Neil was "doing his own thing," way out in the middle of the Pacific Ocean.

My rebellion, which was totally unconscious at the time, was against the worldview in which I had been raised and had bought into in its totality. Worldview is a term in philosophy used to describe the entirety of how you see the world, incorporating your culture, ethnicity, social status, economic situation, theology, political assumptions and moral compass. It encompasses how you see the world, how you think the world operates, why you think things happen as they do and what the meaning and purpose of life is.

Growing up, I bought fully into the "apple pie" philosophy of the American way of life. I was well behaved at school, got almost all A's, played hard in sports, sang in choir, played in the band, was a Cub Scout and Boy Scout, always went to church, read my Bible, prayed every day, was respectful of my elders and I tried to live a moral life. Even after the deaths of my parents I persisted in what we considered to be the "honorable" way of being a Christian and a citizen.

All this changed in college. Because I believed that God causes everything to happen just as it happens, God had thus caused my parents to die. At an emotional and spiritual level, I felt anger at God. However, being angry at God was deeply frowned upon in the religious culture in which I was raised.

Without knowing it, college became my time to cast away this worldview that was no longer working for me. Like so many people, I had made the mistake of believing that if I were a "good boy" my life would go well. Now that my life was not going well, it meant either that I was not a good boy or my worldview was faulty. Fortunately for me, I was coming to see the truth of the latter. As I cast off worship, Bible study and Christian theology classes, I was beginning the search for a worldview and theology that would make more sense to me. In a way, I was just like Job in the Bible, angry at God because he feels God has not lived up to God's part of the bargain, i.e., that if you are a good person, you will be rewarded.

Looking back, I realize how fortunate I was that this internal struggle was taking place within the relatively safe confines of the college campus, and I was far from alone in that struggle, as many students were also in the process of reevaluating the worldviews in which they were raised, especially when it came to nationalism, patriotism and war. Many of my peers followed their worldview into the Vietnam War, and it wasn't until they were fighting in the jungles, watching civilians and their buddies being killed, that many of them began to question what their government was telling them about this war. For those peers this really was a life and death situation. I slowly was becoming aware of this at the time, and I felt a deep sadness for those stuck in such danger for such an ambiguous purpose.

However, since I did not understand the cause of the changes I was going through at the time, I had no ability to articulate what was going on in my life to Neil or anyone else. Neil assumed, as many parents do, that I was just arbitrarily deciding to be a "bad boy," rebelling for the sake of rebelling, and he didn't like it at all.

On top of this, my extroverted socializing made him jealous and embarrassed. That summer he invited me to join his softball team. After the games, the fellows would go out for pizza and beer. Neil did not join them, but I did, and he was angry that I would leave him to hang out with "his boys." The fact that there was drinking involved made it even worse.

Then there was a good friend of mine from Bible camp days who was in the Navy, stationed in Honolulu. He would often come over to Neil's apartment where we would stay up late, playing cards, drinking beer and raiding the freezer looking for a late night snack to cook up.

There was also the fact that for the first time we had lots

of opportunities to talk, which often led to arguments. I could see he really disliked the way I was challenging many of our traditional religious beliefs and the politics of our country, especially regarding the Vietnam War and racism.

I noticed as the summer was coming to a close that I was not hearing as much from my rebound girlfriend. When I finally got back to school for my junior year, I found out why. She was involved with another guy.

Here we go again! I'm now 0 and 3.

But at that point, compared with the losses from death that I had already survived, the breakup didn't seem all that tragic. Like a rubber ball, I just bounced right back up and starting surveying the horizon, where my focus landed on Sandra from South Dakota. She would become an important refuge of support regarding what I was about to experience that fall.

Our relationship began just prior to our junior year when we were both counselors for the national youth gathering at Madison Square Garden, which was, once again, filled with progressive ideas. Sixteen thousand youth descended on New York City under the theme, "And We Care" (note the similarity to our North Dakota theme the year before, "People Are Dying, and We Say We Care"). Music was provide by Pete Seeger, and our speakers included Senator George McGovern of South Dakota—who would be the Democratic presidential candidate two years later--and Clyde Bellcourt, from the White Earth Ojibwa Nation in Minnesota, co-founder of the American Indian Movement with Dennis Banks and others. Imagine the disgust of many of the pastors and adult counselors at the nature of the overall program, especially when McGovern told us how much he disliked the phrase, "America, love it or leave it," preferring "Democracy, live it or lose it!"

The year at school started out with plenty of fun and laughs. I moved back in with my buddies, Joel and Stu, this time to a fairly new apartment in south Moorhead. We decided to take turns cooking once a week, which was pretty much an unmitigated disaster. But we enjoyed having our own place where we could host parties and other gatherings.

My favorite story from that year was about Joel's old Ford Falcon. Originally it was painted orange by the North Dakota Highway Department, but then had been repainted green, although you could still see the orange paint here and there. One morning Joel jumped out of bed, late as usual, to drive the mile and a half to school for an exam. Unfortunately, the transmission was stuck in reverse. Genius that Joel is, he decided to take the back roads and drive to school in reverse. He actually made it in time for the test. Later, when I asked him how the drive went, he replied: "Fine, but my neck got a little sore!"

It did not take long for the fun to end that fall. Losses come in so many different shapes and forms and they each affect us differently, but they also each affect, in big and small ways, the way we understand the world, God and our search for meaning. I was about to experience a new kind of loss: the death of a very close friend.

On October 29, 1970, I received a shocking phone call. My dear friend, Pat Stromswold, had been killed in a car accident in Minneapolis. I was asked to be one of her pallbearers. I shivered with emotions I could not sort out in any way. I was being asked to carry to the grave a good friend whom I loved.

One of the marvelous things about college is the various groups of friends you make, and I had by now been a part of several of those groups. One of them included Pat. She was beautiful, kind, funny, compassionate and just a joy to be around. She was two years older than me, and I had gotten to know her well the previous year when I was a sophomore and she was a senior.

A group of us hung out often and partied together. In those groupings sometimes the boundary between friendship and dating is pretty blurry. Pat and I had mainly been friends, but had gone out a couple of times. Sometimes we would just hang out and read poetry together. During my college years I had collected most of Rod McKuen's books of poetry, and I had shared them with Pat.

As soon as I heard of Pat's death I remembered that I had several letters from her, and I quickly searched to find them. The first one had been written to me in Maddock during the previous Christmas vacation, inviting me to come down to her hometown of Appleton, Minnesota, which is 140 miles south of Concordia. She had signed the letter, "Love You Always, Pat." I had not taken her up on the invitation because I had gone to visit Laura.

The second one had been written the evening of March 17, 1970. I had gone to her dorm to visit that evening, during which we had consumed coffee and read McKuen's poems. She had kept reading McKuen after I left, writing to thank me for coming over, and then quoting another poem he wrote as song lyrics:

> I'll catch the sun and never give it back again.
> I'll catch the sun and keep it for my own.
> And in a world where no one understands
> I'll take my outstretched hand and offer it to anyone
>   who comes along and tells me he's in need of
> love.
>   In need of hope, or maybe just a friend.
>   Perhaps in time I will even share my sun with that
>   new anyone to whom I give my hand. [2]

And then Pat added: "Here's to hoping we never find a world where no one understands—in any case, for you, there's always me." She ended the letter by thanking me for coming over to visit, and then wrote: "Bear, don't stop loving and caring, Pat."

The next letter was sent to me early in June in Hawaii. Pat was working that summer in Fargo-Moorhead and getting ready to graduate the end of June.

The final letter was written August 3 to Hawaii, arriving just after I had left, and forwarded to me in Maddock. She was

---

[2] Rod McKuen, "I'll Catch the Sun," Greatest Hits, Volume 1.

finishing up work in Fargo-Moorhead and getting ready to move to a small town in Minnesota for a teaching job. She ended her letter: "Take care, Bear, you already know I love you, and really miss you a whole lot . . . See you when I get back up here (to Concordia) sometime. Love you, Pat."

I had looked forward to her visiting the old gang at Concordia that fall, but it never happened. Once again death had inserted its ugly head, taking someone dear to me.

How strange it felt as our friendship circle traveled to Appleton to meet Pat's family and friends. First we gathered in her house, looking at the pictures and other remembrances that are always a part of the family home.

Then we drove the short distance to Zion Lutheran Church for the funeral service. The Scripture reading was one that from that day would become my favorite Psalm, 121:

> I will lift up mine eyes unto the hills, from whence cometh my help.
> My help cometh from the Lord, which made heaven and earth.
> The Lord is thy keeper: the Lord is thy shade upon thy right hand.
> The sun shall not smite thee by day, nor the moon by night.
> The Lord shall preserve thee from all evil;
> He shall preserve thy soul.
> The Lord shall preserve thy going out and thy coming in from
> this time forth, and even for evermore. [RSV]

It was time to fulfill our duty as pallbearers. I remembered how we had picked pallbearers for Dad's and Mom's funerals. I knew what an honor it was to be chosen for that duty. And, yes, I was honored to be chosen. But this was an honor I did not want, nor did the others.

We hoisted Pat onto our shoulders, carried her to her grave and set her down to be lowered into it. And again, those words that I, against my will, was getting to know by heart.

"Ashes to ashes, dust to dust, earth to earth!"

As I wrote earlier, our losses can be either regarding that which is precious and now is gone, or that which we wish we had experienced, and never did. With Pat's death I felt both. And I felt that sense of waste that comes when someone so young and so vibrant is ripped from us.

Reading her letters again, almost 50 years later, reminds me of the everlasting beauty and power of love. As McKuen wrote:

> No map to help us find the tranquil flat lands,
> clearings
> calm, fields without mean fences.
> Rolling down the other side of life our compass is the
> sureness of ourselves.
> Time may make us rugged, ragged round the edges,
> but
> know and understand that love is still the safest
> place to land.

One week after Pat's funeral, I received another extremely difficult phone call. A friend--just one year younger than me--from Luther League, had committed suicide. Three days later I would find myself traveling to another small, Minnesota town for a funeral.

I can still remember entering the house and having absolutely no idea what to say. I was in shock. This friend was so bright and so compassionate and had so much to offer the world, and I was not able in any way to begin to wrap my head around what would cause him to take his life. It felt like such a waste. I felt so sad. And I felt such a deep sadness for his family, as they tried to deal with their terrible sense of confusion and loss.

Yes, I had no words, but I did sense that it meant a lot to his family that so many of his friends from Luther League had come for the funeral. Again I experienced the power of presence and empathy in the face of unbelievable loss.

It was then that I experienced another loss, one of a

quite different kind, but very painful, nonetheless. Apparently Neil had had enough of me that summer. My marching against and protesting the Vietnam War, my views on racism and homosexuality, my partying lifestyle: it was too much for him. He had obviously been brooding over my lifestyle and views that fall, and by November decided to abruptly break the silence.

He notified me by letter that he was disowning me and did not want to have anything to do with me again. If that was not bad enough, he wrote letters to Ansel and Dorothy and Pastor Elmo chastising them for not having guided me properly.

I was absolutely incensed, and embarrassed, as was Alan! Neil was our legal guardian, but he had chosen to go off and live in his paradise of Hawaii, leaving our emotional support to folks back in Maddock! They had given that support far in excess of what might be reasonably expected. And now he had the gall to criticize Ansel and Dorothy at the same time they were grieving the loss of their own son, one of Neil's classmates, which you would never have known from his lack of empathy and compassion!

I was thrown into weeks of emotional confusion, really not knowing what to do. In fact, I can't remember much about those days.

Looking through my letters, I found one from Neil dated January 5, 1971. Apparently he had written me a letter on Christmas Day continuing to berate me, and trying to explain his reasons for doing so. I had called him on January 4, and he noted that my voice broke at the beginning of the call, which to him was a positive sign because he took that to mean I must have still cared about our relationship.

There was another letter dated June 27, 1971, which referred to another phone call from me, and another dated September 18, 1971, in which he mentions not having heard from the Hauknesses since his confrontation of them the previous Fall. Duh!

These letters have a strange ambience. On the one hand he grieves the breakdown of the relationship of the three brothers, pointing out how disappointed our parents would be, and at the same time keeps justifying his actions based on what he considers to be the "truth" of his accusations. There is no sense of "agreeing to disagree" for the sake of the relationship.

Now, I admit that, at first, I thought this was a little melodramatic. After all, lots of my progressive friends were having conflict with their parents, and with siblings, especially those in military service. I assumed he was exaggerating, and would eventually get over it.

However, I would be proven wrong. He was serious about severing our relationship, and I was thrust into a period of confusion and hurt that would last for years, and in some ways was never fully resolved.

From the time Neil disowned me, it would be nearly seven years before I would see him again, during which time there was next to no communication from him. That November I was not invited to his wedding and I would not meet his wife for another 6 years. The next time I would see Neil was the summer of 1977.

At the beginning I didn't realize how severe this loss would be. However, as the years dragged on with no or little contact, the pain, frustration and feeling of helplessness increased.

I had had enough of painful events of tragedy and loss, and I turned increasingly inward on my spiritual journey. I resigned from the Student Senate, was no longer President of our synod Luther League and I wasn't going to regular church worship. Activism would have to take a back seat for a period of time.

Sometimes in the spiritual journey you have to turn inward before you can again turn outward. Many spiritual writers, including Henri Nouwen and Thomas Merton, write that one must be comfortable in solitude before one can go actively into the world with compassion. That was also true of Jesus, who began his ministry by spending 40 days alone in the wilderness east of the Jordan River and regularly throughout his ministry tried to get away from his disciples and the crowds to meditate, reflect and pray.

I threw myself into my major areas of study: philosophy, sociology, Christian ethics and world religions. I took some of my classes by independent study, which allowed me to pursue topics in greater depth, and several of my classes were small seminars that allowed and encouraged discussion and challenge to and from fellow students.

My spiritual rebirth was in full swing. I had realized that the only way I could recommit myself to Christianity was not by delving deeper into it, but by leaving it behind, exploring the insights of philosophy and the other great religions of the world and then coming back to it to see if it made any sense. And leave it behind I did. I did not attend worship at church and I did not attend daily chapel at Concordia, except when I was asked to preach. How pompous is that!

Not only did I read and study and discuss the original sources of philosophy and world religions, but also I found great insights in secondary sources, especially the writings on Eastern mysticism by Alan Watts, and amazing novels like Herman Hesse's Siddhartha. Near the end of that novel, Siddhartha (whose name means "achieving that which was searched for") says to his friend, Govinda (also a searcher):

> Knowledge can be communicated, but not wisdom . . . I suspected this when I was still a youth and it was this that drove me away from teachers . . .There is one thought I have had: . . . that is, in every truth the opposite is equally true. For example, a truth can only be expressed and enveloped in words if it is one-sided. Everything that is thought and expressed in words is one-sided, only half the truth; it all lacks totality, completeness, unity. When the Illustrious Buddha taught about the world, he had to divide it . . . into illusion and truth, into suffering and salvation . . . But the world itself, being in and around us, is never one-sided. Never is a man or a deed wholly . . . a saint or a sinner. This only seems so because we suffer the illusion that time is real. Time is not real, Govinda. I

have realized this repeatedly. And if time is not real,
then the dividing line that seems to lie between this
world and eternity, between suffering and bliss,
between good and evil, is also an illusion. [p. 115]

I was weary of those who tried to paint a black and white world, where everything and everyone is labeled as good or evil. This leads to poverty, racism, violence and war. I was searching for a new way of seeing the world, with nuance that realized the ways in which people are alike and can be unified in a common purpose and understanding.

Of course, Luther also wrote that humans are saint and sinner at the same time, but, like I said, I had to leave Christianity behind before I could come back and discover (or rediscover) the truths within it.

My friend Sandra continued to be a great support and we had many wonderful times together. Then something happened, something I still feel somewhat badly about. I was about to find out that, while being dropped by someone can be extremely painful, being on the other side of the equation is no picnic either.

As a freshman, after Pauline, the next woman I had been interested in was a woman from Minnesota named Michelle. She was beautiful, easygoing, fun loving, smart and very talented. The problem was, she was always going with someone else.

Over time we became good friends, and even worked together on some campus activities. My big break came at Christmas, 1970. She finally broke up with her boyfriend, and I pounced. Who is able to untangle the sticky, always spreading, spider web of attraction and affection? I felt badly breaking up with Sandra, but I felt strongly drawn towards Michelle.

After that breakup, everything felt like it was finally falling into place. In a strange way it was a relief not to have to deal with Neil's passive-aggressive (and not always so passive) ways of trying to get me to change. I was fully immersed in my studies, and I was now dating one of my favorite people in the world.

However, life never seems to quit throwing us curveballs. "I just can't catch a break." That is one of our most common experiences in life. One bad thing seems to follow another. Fortunately, there are also times in life when something bad is followed by something good. And then there are those rare times when something good is followed by something even better, something fantastic!

That was about to happen to me.

Part II

Seasons of Life and Love

Chapter 5   Spring

COME, my beloved: let us walk amidst the knolls,
For the snow is water, and Life is alive from its
Slumber and is roaming the hills and valleys.
Let us follow the footprints of Spring into the
Distant fields, and mount the hilltops to draw
Inspiration high above the cool green plains.

The sprigs of grapevine embrace each other like
Sweethearts, and the brooks burst out in dance
Between the rocks, repeating the song of joy;
And the flowers bud suddenly from the heart of
Nature, like foam from the rich heart of the sea.

Come, my beloved; let us drink the last of Winter's
Tears from the cupped lilies, and sooth our spirits
With the shower of notes from the birds, and wander
In exhilaration through the intoxicating breeze.
Let us sit by that rock, where violets hide; let us
Pursue their exchange of the sweetness of kisses.
--Kahlil Gibran

My beloved speaks and says to me: "Arise, my love, my fair
one, and come away; for now the winter is past, the rain is
over and gone. The flowers appear on the earth; the time of
singing has come, and the voice of the turtledove is heard in
our land. The fig tree puts forth its figs, and the vines are in
blossom; they give forth fragrance. Arise, my love, my fair one,
and come away."
--Song of Solomon 2:10-13

"Thanks so much for hosting a party. I hope you don't mind our dropping in."

My head popped up. It wasn't the words that startled me. It was the voice.

Sure enough, when I looked up I saw Pauline and her roommate, Mary, at the door of a friend's basement apartment. It was a typical Friday night social gathering, near the beginning of March, and Michelle and I had arrived about a half hour earlier.

I hadn't seen Pauline for months. Since that fateful night in the fall of my freshman year when she stood me up, I occasionally ran into her on campus. However, in December I had heard through the grapevine that she had become quite ill and had been sent to the University of Minnesota Hospitals for testing and treatment. At the time I had called Pauline's roommate, Mary, to find out what was going on. She told me that Pauline had had a seizure and eventually had to drop out of school and move back home to live with her parents in Bismarck.

What happened next is pretty much a blur, filled with a bit of embarrassment. Either Pauline came and sat next to me or I sat by her, but we spent the rest of the evening catching up. You would have thought we were the closest, life-long friends. The embarrassment is that I no doubt neglected Michelle the rest of the evening.

I don't like to think of myself as impulsive, but what would you say about a fellow who had coffee with Pauline the very next morning, and then the following day told Michelle I was ending our relationship so I could be with Pauline. I must have been out of my mind, or smitten beyond rationality, or Pauline and I were at a stage in life where we both knew what we wanted, and that included each other. I imagine it was some combination of all of those things.

Looking back, it still seems to me like one of the strangest things. After all those relationships where I insecurely wondered if the other person cared as much about me as I them, I now walked into a relationship where that really never crossed my mind. And to think it was with a woman who had dropped me like a sack of spuds.

With Laura, I had thought we were meant to be, and was sadly mistaken. With Pauline, I had assumed we would never be, and here we were together again, ready in one weekend to begin rebuilding our relationship.

I think when we met as frosh we were each looking to find our stride, and we wanted to explore the myriad of new relationships and areas of study that had now opened up for us. Now, two and half years later, we had both had the chance to do that and we had matured into adults ready to begin making long term decisions about what we wanted to do with our lives.

I was crazy about Pauline, and had never stopped being so, but now our relationship didn't feel unbalanced or unequal, where I feared she would drop me again. We were both ready to make a commitment to one another and we both just seemed to know that we were right for each other.

So, about me being impulsive. All I did was drop Michelle, call the Bible camp in California to renege on the contract I had signed to be the Program Director for the coming summer and made plans to follow Pauline to Wisconsin, where she planned to live with her sister for the summer. I rented a room on a farm and spend the summer working construction during the week and pumping gas on the weekends.

I really don't remember much about that spring. I was busy finishing up classes and Pauline, even though she was not back in school, spent most of the spring staying with Mary in their old apartment, giving us lots of time to be together.

That was the apartment in which that spring Pauline's former boyfriend would come over and try to beat me up so I could practice my non-violent tactics, finally saved by the clawing, screaming and hitting of Pauline and Mary as they pulled him off my back.

That was also the spring when Pauline, Mary and I headed out for a drive in my prized Ford Maverick, and, trying to make a difficult left turn on to Highway 75, I would pull out and before I could cross the second lane be T-boned by a speeding car, throwing us violently into the ditch. Mary sustained a gash on her face but, apart from being shaken up, no serious damage was done to any of us. We were extremely lucky, or blessed, or both. My car was totaled. If the other car had hit a couple of feet toward me, I would have been . . . well, I really don't like to think about it.

Now I had no car, and no way to get to Wisconsin. Eventually I hitchhiked to Bismarck and Pauline's dad took me to his favorite car dealer. They put me in a 1964 blue Plymouth Belvedere with push button transmission, which was all I could afford with the $400 I had pulled together, not having been able to afford collision insurance on my new Maverick.

However, that car was enough to get Pauline and me to Williams Bay, Wisconsin. That summer I worked a lot of hours and Pauline spent her days with her sister, Gail, who was pregnant. We managed to squeeze in dates here and there between my two jobs.

At the end of the summer, on the way back to Concordia, we spent a few days in Minneapolis, staying with Pauline's other sister, Carole, where I took a short bartending course so that I could find a good paying job when I returned to school for my senior year.

I quickly found the perfect position bartending at the Lamplighter Inn in Moorhead, Minnesota, and it was there, on my 21st birthday, surrounded by several friends, that we announced our engagement to be married the following spring after I had graduated.

Pauline decided to spend the year in Bismarck, living at home and taking courses at Bismarck State College, although she came down to visit whenever she could and I visited her every holiday. I worked long hours bartending and saved as much as I could for graduate school. I was very focused at school, as all of my classes were now in my major fields, although much of our energy went into planning our wedding, and for me, trying to decide whether to apply to seminary or graduate school in theology.

I was still feeling uneasy about being a pastor, but I was now taking several courses in Christian ethics and feeling more comfortable in the church. I was leaning towards going to graduate school in theology, and two of my religion professors encouraged me to apply to the University of Chicago Divinity School.

What I did next is still a mystery to me. Anyone who has ever applied to law school or any graduate program knows that, in addition to applying to a favored school or two, you also apply to schools that may not be at the top of your list, but where you have a better chance of being accepted.

But not me! I applied to my favorite school, and that school only. When the University of Chicago did not accept my application, I had nowhere else to turn. So I looked into seminary.

I told my professors that if I were to go to seminary I wanted to do so in a place that would expand my horizon beyond the Norwegian/German culture in which I had been raised and gone to school. Again they pointed me to Chicago, to the Lutheran School of Theology, which is on the south side of Chicago, some seven miles from downtown. I did get accepted there, and began making plans to start classes in the fall of 1972.

On April 30, 1972, I graduated from Concordia College Magna Cum Laude. Neil was not there, but my brother Alan, Pauline and her parents, Dorothy and Ansel, and Pastor Elmo and Norma Anderson all attended. As one last act of campus resistance, many of us graduates wore black armbands to protest the ROTC Commissioning that was allowed to be a part of our graduation ceremonies-- not because we were opposed to the military itself, but because we did not feel our graduation ceremony should imply support for U.S. military involvement in Vietnam.

Pauline presented me with a graduation card after the ceremony, which read: "I love you, Bear, with my heart so filled with love for you I am wordless. Forever I will be standing at your side, through proud moments like this or sorrowful times, as long as God permits."

A week later, on May 6, 1972, all of the same people, along with many others, gathered around Pauline and me at Trinity Lutheran Church in Bismarck to be married. Everything was beautiful and romantic; except that when Pauline and I finally left the church reception we found that my friends had hoisted my old Plymouth up on blocks, higher than my jack could reach. Fortunately, the pastor who married us had an extra tall jack, and was able to lower our car to the ground.

We set out westward for our honeymoon, driving through Montana, Colorado, Nevada and California. From there we headed up one of the most beautiful drives in the world, the Pacific Coast Highway. However, my joy did not last long. Out of nowhere I had my first, and thank God, my last abscessed tooth. I forced my way into a dentist office where I was told I needed a root canal. Once I heard the price, and informed the dentist I had neither insurance nor money, but an unbearable amount of pain, I was able to convince him to simply yank the tooth out, which he did. Finally we arrived, one tooth less, at Mt. Cross Bible Camp near Santa Cruz, California, where, one year delayed, I would finally be the Program Director for the summer.

Pauline and I really enjoyed our first summer of marriage. After all of my years working at Bible camps, the work came quite easily to me. I especially enjoyed mentoring the camp staff, sharing insights and skills I had learned throughout the years as a staff member myself.

August brought a return trip to North Dakota, where we visited our families and then loaded a U-Haul trailer, attached it to the back of our trusty Plymouth, and headed to Chicago.

We moved into seminary student housing, which was a beautiful, old row house apartment, with four locks on the front door, in one of the poorest areas of Chicago. Our neighbor informed us that the night before someone had been shot and killed right in front of our apartment.

At that point Pauline's parents, who had helped us move, were starting to have second thoughts about her matrimonial partner. I assured them that I would take care of her, until death do us part, but added that I was quite sure that would be quite a ways down the road. Of course, I was basically whistling in the dark, but love makes you say the strangest things.

Pauline, with what little money we had, decided to make our apartment real "mod." We painted the whole place black, white and red, and pulled together an ugly, grey hide-a-bed from the Petersons, that weighed about a 1000 pounds, with some cheap, plastic furniture to create our first home. We put rabbit ears on an old black and white TV and were thrilled by all the stations available in Chicago.

What is it about your first home? It really doesn't matter where it is, or what furnishings you have. It is such a delight to do whatever you can to make the space comfortable, welcoming and livable. More than once over the years I have created an end table with a cardboard box covered with a cloth. I have built a bar in the same fashion. I have made bookcases out of scraps of wood and concrete blocks. Before long, Pauline and I had created a space that felt safe and warm, with the final touch being the arrival of Pauline's brown, tabby cat from Bismarck, Tuna, and the purchase of a black and white kitten, Sammy.

I turned an old porch area into my study, tried to start school with a positive attitude and we settled in to our new life together. Frankly, I was beginning seminary on a trial basis. I had decided to give it a year and see how it went. I was quite sure I would enjoy the study of theology, but I wasn't at all sure I was up to the pastoral ministry skills that would also need to be learned and practiced. The "trial basis" thus had two dimensions to it: both the theological/philosophic and the practical.

Having majored in philosophy and world religions in college, I had seen the relativity of the doctrine I had always been told was absolute truth. I was intrigued by the "orthodox fallacy," which is the presupposition that whatever one believes is the standard by which the rest of the world shall be judged. I thus wondered if my faith was, so to speak, firm and strong enough to make me both worthy of and successful at being a parish pastor.

Secondly, having worked at Bible camps for five summers and being very involved in Luther League for several years, I had met and witnessed the work of many pastors. As mentioned previously, I was not entirely impressed by all of them, but, fortunately, there were some who were great guides and an inspiration to me. Nevertheless, I wasn't at all sure I wanted to cast my lot with this vocation and I started seminary not knowing if I was called to parish ministry.

I wasn't excited about delving into the common areas of seminary study, like Bible and church history. However, in my first semester I was thrust into a new area of theology that would significantly change my thinking, and also my sense of calling to be a pastor, and that was a course titled Systematic Theology I. Systematic Theology is where you--so to speak-- "construct" your own theological "system," using what you know about the Bible, church history and doctrine, the practical areas of ethics and social ministry and your own experience both within and outside the church.

The first step in doing this is by studying the theological systems of other theologians, with a focus on their methodology, (i.e., what principles do they use to pull together all the areas mentioned above). In my time at seminary I studied historical theologians like Aquinas and Martin Luther, but also contemporaries, who at the time included Paul Tillich, Karl Barth, Rudolph Bultmann, and Reinhold and H. Richard Niebuhr. Of the various categories of study, the ones that interested me most were Christology (the study of Christ), Ecclesiology (the study of the church), Soteriology (the study of salvation), and Theological Anthropology (what does it mean to be human?).

I was also fascinated by the research of my professor, Carl E. Braaten, in the area of theology we call Eschatology (the study of the end times). I was quickly mesmerized, not only by his grasp of theology, but also by the "Theology of Hope" constructed by German theologians Wolfhart Pannenberg and Jürgen Moltmann. What I found in this theology of hope was two ways of understanding Christianity that not only made sense to me, but gave me hope for the future, both for my own life and for the life of the world. This came through a new way of viewing the meaning of cross and resurrection.

The cross is God's way of identifying with the pain of the world, with the great suffering that we all experience. It is God's way of showing us both that God cares about our pain, and, more so, that God is willing to enter into it with us. This is the theological equivalent of what I had already experienced in my times of loss and grief: the presence of another in the midst of grief brings a strange but very real kind of comfort, and thereby hope.

Furthermore, our hope for healing comes not through looking back to the past, but through anticipating the future. Much of traditional theology has been focused on Repristination, which is the attempt to restore something to its original state or condition. The Garden of Eden was perfect, and our task now is to get back to that state. This locks us into the belief that the best we can hope for in the future is to return to the best of what we have already experienced.

The Theology of Hope, on the other hand, looks to the future, believing and trusting that God can do a new thing different from what has ever happened before. God is the power of creativity and redemption, in ways far beyond what we might imagine. In the words of Moltmann, "Believing in the resurrection does not just mean assenting to a dogma and noting a historical fact. It means participating in this creative act of God . . . Resurrection is not consoling opium, soothing us with the promise of a better world in the hereafter. It is the energy for a rebirth of this life. The hope doesn't point to another world. It is focused on the redemption of this one." [3]

I began to slowly realize that so much of my focus was on the past, on what had already happened in my life. I felt guilt about abandoning Dad and anger at Mom for abandoning me. I kept wishing my life had been different, and that I had

---

[3] Jürgen Moltmann, Jesus Christ for Today's World, trans. By Margaret Kohl (Minneapolis: Fortress Press, 1994), p. 80, 81.

done things differently in the past.

Now I began to see that healing would come not through struggling to redeem the past, but by trusting that God had new things in store for me. I began to see God as the power of hope that could bring healing and change to my life and to the world.

As the weeks went by I realized that I was really excited about my new life. The deeper I got into theology the more passion I felt about it. And, when I wasn't in class or studying, life with Pauline was perfect. Well, almost.

University of Minnesota doctors had diagnosed Pauline's illness as primary pulmonary hypertension of the lungs, a rare disease of unknown origin characterized by deterioration of the arteries in the lungs. Over time this condition causes the heart to overwork and enlarge as it struggles to pump blood through increasingly smaller arteries.

Pauline's condition was complicated by neurological problems related to the insufficient oxygenation of her blood, producing seizures, double vision, dizziness and headaches. It became very difficult for her to read for extended periods, which is why she had dropped out of school after her first seizure at Concordia.

Pauline told me everything she knew about her condition. However, she felt that her doctors had been somewhat vague, probably because it is very difficult to give an exact prognosis for the disease. Cases vary greatly from person to person.

This was also in the day when doctors tended to be less honest with their patients. You were not allowed to see your own medical records and there was no WebMD for analyzing your symptoms.

Typical of two young people in love, we tried to ignore and repress the truth about Pauline's illness. Her lung condition did not restrict her greatly as long as she didn't run, walk long flights of stairs or do any other strenuous physical activity. We hoped, as most people who face serious illness do, that a cure would be found eventually.

Our immediate concern focused on her neurological

problems, which were severe enough that she was pretty sure she could not handle a job, even though we were very short on money. She wanted to go back to school, preferably to get a degree in social work, but was not confident her neurological problems would allow it. She also wanted to have children, but her doctors feared that childbirth would be fatal due to the intense strain it would put on her heart.

Many of our conversations during that first year of marriage were about these issues. Like many men tend to do, I probably did not listen closely enough to her concerns and jumped too quickly into trying to reassure her. I told her that since leaving Maddock I had lived on a meager budget, and I had no trouble doing that again. At the risk of sounding like that pained parent who talks about walking miles to school each day, both ways uphill, we found a way to make two meals out of a can of tuna and four out of a pound of hamburger. I am quite sure there must have been a lot of noodles and cream of mushroom soup involved.

Nevertheless, Pauline struggled during these days with her identity and self-worth. She often experienced guilt because she felt she wasn't contributing meaningfully to society or financially to our marriage.

As much as she could Pauline liked to read, and write letters to her family and friends. She also liked to keep the house neat and clean, and to cook when she felt well enough to do so. We loved our evenings having dinner together, then talking or watching TV. We also began to develop friendships with other students, and soon weekends including social gatherings with them.

Our outings included a couple of local restaurants, but our favorite date was to hop on Lake Shore Drive and head north along Lake Michigan through beautiful, downtown Chicago, ending up at Old Town, where there were two restaurants we really enjoyed.

However, the activity we enjoyed most was having long talks over a soda, beer or glass of wine. Because of my studies and Pauline's interests our conversations—long into the night—often centered on theology, our hopes and dreams for the future and the meaning of faith.

It was during these long discussions that I began to realize just how "pure" Pauline's faith was (much more so than mine). Not that it was simple, or naïve. By no means! Pauline loved theology, and she wasn't afraid to share her questions or doubts. Indeed, both of us believed that doubt was not the antithesis of faith, but part of the struggle of faith. Even so, there was always something so trusting, so accepting about her faith. Doubt never threw her into depression or the kind of questioning that leaves one feeling insecure. For her, trust seemed to come easily.

Psychologically, we call such trust peace of mind. Theologically, we call it grace. Pauline accepted it as a gift, trusting her life and future into the loving hands of God.

In the search for some income while I was studying, I came across a wonderful opportunity. A shipping company on the west side of Chicago had an arrangement with a number of my fellow seminary students. They employed teamsters to load semi-trailers, which were then shipped by rail to the west coast. If they did not get their docks cleared on Friday, they brought their workers back on Saturday morning at time and a half pay. Sometimes they had so many inventories they brought in extras: namely, we seminary students.

The unpleasant part was I wouldn't know if I would be working until I heard the phone ring at 6 that morning. That's when they would call if they needed workers, and we had to be there by 7 am. The good part was the pay was $10 an hour, which seemed monstrous as compared to the construction job I'd worked two summers before for $2 an hour.

In spite of this job, by the time my first year of seminary ended, we were broke. I talked to the shipping company and they hired me on the management side to prepare invoices for the workers on the dock. I spent the next year working the graveyard shift, from midnight to 8 am. Believe me, one year of doing that was enough; more than enough. It made going to school look like a picnic.

Typically I would stay awake until 9:30 to 10:00 pm, then

take a nap until 11:30 pm, getting up in time to drive to work. Pauline was a real night owl, and she would stay up reading or watching TV until 4 am, at which time I would call her so we could talk over my lunch break. She would then go to bed, I would finish my shift, drive home, have breakfast and head to bed and sleep until late afternoon.

In addition to saving money from my work that year, we also began to receive another form of income. Because of Pauline's health problems, a government official in Bismarck who knew her dad suggested that she apply for disability income through a government program called Supplemental Security Income, or SSI. Working with her doctors she was eventually granted acceptance, and although the monthly checks were quite small, they definitely helped.

During her long hours in the evenings and nights alone, Pauline watched television, read as much as she could, reflected and began to journal.

Despite her frustration with headaches and not being able to do many of the things she wanted to do, Pauline compensated quite well, celebrating the good things in her life. On November 18, 1973, she wrote:

> It's been a great day. I feel very happy and lucky, and just thrilled to be alive . . . This afternoon we watched football (which I am beginning to enjoy), went down by the lake (it was a beautiful fall day, and not windy; the lake was so calm and pretty), ate at the Surf and Surrey Restaurant and took a walk down to our little shopping center where I bought this notebook. Bear's at work now so it's lonesome, but nice lonesome. Sammy (our cat) is sleeping at my feet to keep me company, and Bear is with me in mind. I love this time of night, so peaceful, and quiet, yet so loving and warm.

While celebrating the beauty of our springtime love, Pauline recognized life's frailties. The cold, Chicago winter breathing on our door reflected the chilling possibilities of the future. On February 11, 1974 she wrote:

> Right now my mind is troubled. The "Tomorrow Show" was about death. Most of my prayers concern death, or, I should say, the "not death yet" of my loved ones. I'm scared of it; scared Bear will die and I'll feel so all alone; scared Mom and Dad will die and I'll grieve so much, too much; afraid Gail and Carole will die. Now I'm suddenly aware that I myself am scared to die. I don't want to leave Bear, my parents, my family; I'm having such a good time living. Three years ago I didn't feel that way; I just didn't care about myself.

In the midst of this awareness of how transient life is, Pauline described her desire to contribute something meaningful to the world with her life:

> I hope I can do something good with my life . . . It is because   God is with me always that I never have to experience real loneliness. I cannot imagine living without His spirit within you. I fervently hope and pray that Bear and I are capable of spreading His word and love. Nothing else in life is as important to me.

That second year of our marriage Pauline continued to have her neurological problems, along with a new problem. A side effect of Dilantin, which she took to control her seizures, is the swelling of the gums. The only solution is a painful surgery in which the gums are cut back. Lacking dental insurance, we arranged for her to have the work done by a student dentist at the University of Illinois Medical School. The surgery was successful, but also extremely painful, and it was difficult for her to eat for sometime thereafter.

As the year progressed I started to consider whether I should remain at Lutheran School of Theology in Chicago, or transfer to Luther Theological Seminary in St. Paul,

Minnesota. The Chicago school was part of the Lutheran Church in America (LCA), and St. Paul was a school of the American Lutheran Church (ALC), the denomination in which I was raised. These two denominations would eventually merge in 1988, but at that time I had to go to at least one year at an ALC seminary if I was going to be ordained into the ALC.

I could have stayed at Chicago one more year, and transferred for my senior year, but I decided to transfer in the summer of 1974 for my second year of seminary. In fact, we moved at the end of May so I could take summer school at Luther, studying Greek and Hebrew to catch up, since the schools had different requirements. I soon panicked, realizing how far behind in Greek I was, and how difficult Hebrew was. I finally decided to drop Hebrew and start over with beginner Greek at Luther, which would turn out to be one of the smartest decisions I would make.

Soon we were getting to know other students, and Pauline really enjoyed living in the same city as her sister and a close childhood friend.

Luther Seminary was much larger than my previous school, and I enjoyed the greater variety of courses and instructors available. However, it also tended to be more conservative theologically, and far too parochial for me. I was in the process of throwing off the shackles of the traditional, conservative belief that God controls all things and that, therefore, all things are God's will. Additionally, conservatives in the church tended to believe that one should keep theology and politics separate. I, on the other hand, had spent a good deal of my studies in college focusing on Christian ethics, including the role of the church in influencing government when it came to issues of war, violence, human rights and the equality of women, gays and all races of people. I frequently found myself in conflict with other students and a few of the faculty.

This created some real problems for me, as I was raised to avoid conflict at all costs, and it took: I have always disliked conflict and have had to learn, painfully, how to be confrontational when it is necessary. But I also have a lot of passion, and am equally uncomfortable sitting on the sidelines quietly when I disagree with a theological position or an ethical or political position.

As I was working at trying to find my place and stride at this new seminary, Pauline continued to struggle with her sense of vocation and the meaning of life. On October 21, 1974, she wrote in her journal:

> I've been thinking often of myself, and feeling so worthless. I want to accomplish something, do something, be something, help somebody. Every night I pray for God to help me—but what a cop-out. I'm the one who has to go out and find what I need. I have to do it. I can't expect God to one day hand me something meaningful.

Pauline did not waste time in doing just that. She joined a group called "Seminary Wives" to make friends and audited classes in pastoral care. This in turn led to her doing volunteer pastoral care a few hours a week at a nursing home for young people with diseases such as multiple sclerosis, muscular dystrophy and cerebral palsy. This experience reinforced Pauline's desire to be a social worker.

As the year unfolded Pauline began to reflect on the suffering she had gone through and the way in which it had brought her to new awareness of the meaning and purpose of her life. On February 7, 1975 she wrote:

> I just thought of a major plus in my getting sick. I've been depressed now and then thinking of my first reaction at the University of Minnesota Hospital. Honestly, I wasn't upset about being ill, nor was I extremely worried that the diagnosis would be ultra-black. The reason? I didn't care. I wasn't at all concerned. For if I found I had something terminal, that would have been too bad, but . . . apathy on my part. However, to even reach that point one must examine her life—all the good and bad acts, her

reason for living, her kindness. Slowly, very slowly did I begin, or at least try, to change myself, alter my feelings, and quit living just for myself.

Two months later I was submitted to another diagnosis. And this time I fervently prayed that everything would be found okay. In just two short months I wanted to live—I was happy with myself. True, my personal life had changed so much for the better. I was in love and the love was returned. However, that wasn't all of it. I had starting liking myself.

No longer am I upset at my original apathy. I needed it, needed going through the pain of wondering why, so I could be a complete and happy person today. I now love, love myself, love my husband, love God. I want to go to others. Perhaps I can make some slight contribution to this world.

In late March we finally received word on Steven Haukness. The previous August a gravesite had been found in Vietnam, and on March 23, 1975 (7 years after his disappearance) Steven's remains were identified. On April 4 a memorial service was held at North Viking, and Steven was buried in the Haukness burial plot, right next to my parents. Although the discovery of the gravesite and the identification of Steven's remains did not really surprise us, it did dash the faint hopes we still carried that he might be alive and threw us back into another painful experience of loss.

My first school year at Luther flew by and it was time for my third year of seminary, which included a quarter of what is called Clinical Pastoral Education (CPE) at a hospital, and then a year-long internship in a congregation. I was not able to find a CPE site in Minneapolis/St. Paul and ended up heading to Boston for the summer to develop my pastoral care skills.

The biggest challenge we faced was Pauline's

neurological problems. Her headaches and double vision were especially bad that summer. Pauline was also lonely and we weren't in Boston long enough for her to get involved in any kind of volunteer activities. This would normally not have been a problem, because Pauline loved to read and journal. However, that summer she was limited in her ability to do so, and could not adjust her medications so far from her doctors.

Nevertheless, the summer was one of continuing self-revelation for Pauline as her love of self and her sense of identity blossomed further. On August 10 she wrote: "I feel wonderful about myself. I feel more secure. I am a bit more aggressive, I definitely do not feel badly that I don't work and I am now able to sometimes get angry at my sickness. It's not my fault."

Meanwhile, I threw myself into the CPE program, which included small group time spent with our CPE supervisor and several other students in the program, representing several different denominational backgrounds. Beyond critiquing our work with patients, we also shared and confronted our own interpersonal dynamics.

That summer I had begun to have a consistent dream about Dad. I would receive the news that I was going to be granted a period of 24 hours to be with him, during which I could discuss anything I wanted. I was elated, and I could barely wait for Dad to appear in the dream. However, each time, just as he was about to appear, I would awaken. I was so disappointed! I felt so empty and helpless! I often found myself in tears.

This dream repeated itself several times, and each time it was almost exactly the same. Finally the day came when it my turn to talk about my family with the CPE group. I decided to start with Dad. As I began to speak, I could feel a surge of emotion welling up from deep inside me. First the tears came, and before long I was convulsing in grief. Then I looked up to the ceiling and addressed Dad: "Dad, I love you! Dad, I'm so sorry I abandoned you. Please forgive me! I need to know so badly that you love me!"

There was a long period of silence, and then the group

got up and gathered around me. Finally one of them verbalized the truth that was so obvious to them, but hidden from me by my guilt: "You know, Brian, you feel you did not love your dad enough to stand by him as he was dying. The truth is you loved him so much you could not bear to see him die."

That was the truth! It took awhile for it to sink in, but it was the truth, and I knew it was the truth. It was the truth, in the words of Jesus, which "set me free."

I have never had that dream again, and, for the most part, I have been able to live the last 40 years without feeling guilty about my last days with my father. Once again I was able to celebrate the wonderful relationship we always had. I would still feel grief about the lack of Dad's presence, but at least that pain of loss was no longer compounded by guilt.

I couldn't wait to race home and share with Pauline the healing I had experienced, and somehow I knew, in addition to my personal happiness, that this experience would make me a better pastor.

It ended up being a wonderful summer for both of us, in spite of Pauline's neurological problems. We quickly learned how to get around town on the rail system and we spent many weekends exploring New England, from the tip of Cape Cod to Bar Harbor, Maine. It was there that we found a beautiful, seaside restaurant on the ocean shore, and, over lobster and wine, talked of the glories of our love and our dreams for the future

As the summer came to a close, we once again packed a U-Haul to head home. We visited the Haukness family at their Minnesota cabin and Pauline's parents in Bismarck before heading to Spokane, Washington, where I would do a year-long internship.

At this point in my spiritual and vocational journey I was really enjoying the study of theology and I had received a great deal of personal insight and affirmation of my pastoral care abilities through CPE, but I was still leery of taking on the role of a parish pastor.

The congregation had provided a small, but cute,

upstairs apartment in an old house whose owner lived below us. With Pauline's breathing problems the stairways up sometimes provided a challenge, but most of the time she managed them quite well. The church was in easy walking distance for me, and the congregation had provided a small study out of which I could carry on my ministry. I preached once a month, led weekly worship, taught new member classes and confirmation and visited many people in hospitals and nursing homes. The greatest amount of my time, however, was spent in youth ministry, which was just fine by me. It was the part of ministry I enjoyed the most after so many years working at Bible camps and in Luther League.

Pauline continued to spend most of her time in our apartment, reading, writing letters and cooking meals. Her doctors had made progress in finding the right balance of medicines and her headaches and vision cooperated quite nicely that year. Most of the time she felt fairly well. She kept finding greater meaning and purpose in life, attending worship, occasionally accompanying me on my pastoral visits and participating in youth ministry events as her health allowed.

Pauline had a special ability to relate with people of all ages. She seemed intuitively to know what was needed in various situations.

One evening we received a call that a woman named Mary, whom we had gotten to know quite well, was in the hospital near death. Pauline insisted on going to the hospital with me.

We talked briefly with several family members. Then, as I stood contemplating what to do next, Pauline quickly walked to Mary's side, took her hand and visited with her. She slowly began to recite the Lord's Prayer, giving Mary plenty of time to say the words with her. When the prayer was finished, Pauline leaned over, kissed Mary and whispered, "I know God is with you."

At first I found myself somewhat bored in my tiny study at church, missing my theology classes and not as excited as I had hoped about reading theology on my own. However, as I received positive feedback on my preaching, teaching and pastoral visitation ministry, I found myself becoming more invested in the congregation in particular, and parish ministry in general. What excited me the most continued to be youth ministry.

Before I arrived, a fairly solid youth ministry program had already been established, and my task was to continue to move that program forward. We already had in place a talented group of high school leaders, and some outstanding parents as advisors. I met with that group on a monthly basis to plan and divide up duties for upcoming events. I learned early on an important lesson that would be key to how I would formulate youth ministry programs in the future.

That key was to heavily involve the youth themselves in the planning of events. I soon found that youth do not always know what they want to do, but they are clear about what they do not want to do. Our task as adults was to suggest possible things we might do, and the youth would quickly let us know what would work and what would not.

Once an event is decided upon, the youth should do most of the implementation. Some would work on the event itself, finding a place, picking a time, figuring out the cost. Others would do the advertising. And, the more youth were involved in putting the event together, the greater the number of youth who would attend because no one wants to plan an event that is a flop, and so the youth were the main ones to encourage their friends to participate.

As the year came to a close all of my reviews, both from the congregation and from the seminary, were very positive. This both excited me and scared me. The fear part had to do with the fact that I was having success, and a fair amount of enjoyment, in a profession I wasn't at all sure I wanted to embrace. It felt like being on a rollercoaster, unable to get off, but also not sure you wanted to ride it to the end.

As the summer ended, out of nowhere I experienced another kind of "coming together." Neil began to write me again. I am not sure what prompted this, and I don't remember exactly when it began. Apparently I had written Neil a letter about my experiences on internship, and he sent a response on July 23, 1976 in which he commented to me about the "confirmation of your vocation" while also stating that he was doing a lot of "soul searching" about his own vocation.

This was followed by two apologies, one having to do with money, and one having to do with his having disowned me.

Mom's will had stated that Brian and Alan should receive a "good education," and then the balance of the estate would be divided three ways equally. Alan and I approached Neil, asking that we continue to receive money from the estate as I went to seminary and he went to law school. Neil objected to this firmly, taking the position that a "good education" only included undergraduate studies.

Through Ansel, Alan and I had a family lawyer and we went to get his opinion. He counseled us that, with the rather small amount of money left in the estate, and Neil taking such a firm stand, it would not be worth the legal fees to challenge his decision as our guardian.

Now, years later, Neil had apparently come to realize that his action was a factor in why I had to take a year off from seminary in Chicago to work to make money, and he wrote that his action likely caused me to "waste a year" and kept me from graduating a year earlier.

Then he went on to his relationship with Alan and me: "I always had the dream that the Erickson brothers would be a special family and have a special relationship. Well, I think I blew that when I decided, for what then I thought was a good reason, to hurt you the way I did early this decade . . . I have never come right out and said it, but I wish you would forgive me for that period, and I am sorry for the troubles I caused you financially, and mentally, and any other way."

As the middle child of three, I have always tried to be the "great mediator," and thus I received Neil's confession positively. I hoped that this could, indeed, be the beginning of a new relationship among all three of us.

And it did seem in many ways to be a new start. Neil was developing a renewed interest in his own Christian faith, and was fascinated by all of the things I was studying in seminary. Over the next couple of years he would often ask me questions about theology or the Bible in his letters, and I would respond as clearly as I could.

In August we packed yet another U-Haul back to Luther Seminary in St. Paul. The return to school for the senior year is very exciting, as you see your classmates for the first time in over a year and you get to hear of the adventures they have had on their internships. Everyone is changed in some way, either moving towards or away from parish ministry.

My own ambivalence about a possible career as a minister would be met almost immediately by a seminary requirement at the beginning of one's senior year. In order to continue with our studies, we had to write a paper explaining our understanding of our call to ministry, which had to, in turn, be approved by the seminary faculty in order to continue on the path to ordained ministry.

At the time of Martin Luther this call referred primarily to the process by which one was ordained for special service in the church. Luther expanded this understanding of call to include all Christians who, through baptism, are called to follow and serve Christ. In the concept of the "priesthood of all believers," he enlarges the understanding of call beyond professional, church ministry. One's calling includes one's work as well as such things as being a spouse, a parent, a person of love who reaches out to those in need.

Nevertheless, to be ordained you are supposed to have experienced, first, some kind of a specific call from God to professional church ministry, and, secondly, the church must also confirm this call. Therefore, to be ordained in the Lutheran church you must demonstrate that you have been called in both senses, and that was the task that lay before me as I started my senior year.

The first dimension, which we think of most often, is a sense or experience of being called by God to a certain kind of ministry or service. This is the kind of call we see throughout the Scriptures, whether it be God calling Jeremiah to be a prophet, Moses to lead the Hebrew people out of slavery in Egypt or Paul to a radical transformation in which he went from persecuting the early Christians to a new ministry calling people to follow Jesus.

The second dimension of call is the confirmation of the church. The church has to be convinced that you have the gifts and skills for ordained ministry. You can be removed from the call process if you don't have adequate academic ability, psychological integration, pastoral skills or sound character.

In my paper I had no problem talking about the generalized call of all the baptized uplifted by Luther. However, when it came to an experience or conviction of being called by God into ordained ministry: well, I was honest and admitted I wasn't sure.

All I could really point to was the second sense of call: the confirmation I had received continually over the years from the people I had worked with who felt I had the gifts for ministry. It was almost as if I was hoping someone else would make the decision for me that I was having difficulty making for myself.

The faculty did eventually approve me for ordination, but I am quite sure it was not unanimous.

Returning to school, I had decided to apply for a special program called Para-Seminary (para in Greek means "with") that would allow me to work several required and elective courses into a special, independent study project that would result in a lengthy paper at its conclusion.

I had continued to study eschatology and the theology of hope at Luther, and wrote a proposal suggesting that I work five courses into a Para-Seminary project on eschatology, which would include biblical studies on how the Gospel writers and St. Paul understood eschatology, and what this might mean for Christian ethics and theology today. I was accepted into the program, which gave me greater excitement for my senior year, although I don't think I was entirely cognizant of what I was getting myself into.

As a major deadline neared around Christmas, I experienced a new phenomenon in my life: persistent insomnia. I would lay awake worrying about whether I would get this project completed, I would wake up tired, have trouble concentrating, and this would, in turn, make me even more worried. This kept increasing my anxiety as I worried that I had taken on a project that, while exciting, could doom my seminary studies and thereby graduation and ordination.

I did the only thing I know how to do in such a situation: put one foot in front of the other, one day at a time, to peck away at what looked to me like a gigantic rock. I got done what needed to be done by Christmas, and that break renewed me in spirit and body. Things would go much better in the New Year and by spring I had completed an over 200-page paper on eschatology and the theology of hope. I argued that no matter what suffering one may be experiencing in the present, God continues to open future possibilities for newness and change. This is the basis of our hope.

Pauline continued auditing courses, doing volunteer visitation and enjoying her time with family and our growing circle of friends. In May I graduated from Luther with the degree of Master of Divinity, and awaited a call to a congregation.

Spring gave way to summer. Our love was in full bloom and we carried in our hearts excitement for the future. Even though summer is obviously closer to winter than spring, winter now seemed far off. Spring comes forth from death, just as the blossoming of love sprouts from loneliness. When summer arrives, and nature is in full bloom, it seems invincible. What can destroy it's pervading beauty!

Pauline set aside her journal for several years. Journaling often grows out of pain and searching. Pauline's energy now went into her ever-widening circles of interest and involvement. My energy went into embracing parish ministry, once and for all, for better or for worse. It was time to dance in the fields of grain and eat the ripened fruit of our love.

Chapter 6   Summer

Let us go into the fields, my beloved, for the
Time of Harvest approaches, and the sun's eyes
Are ripening the grain.

Let us tend the fruit of the earth, as the
Spirit nourishes the grains of Joy from the
Seeds of Love, sowed deep in our hearts.

Let us fill our bins with the products of
Nature, as life fills so abundantly the
Domain of our hearts with her endless bounty.

Let us make the flowers our bed, and the
Sky our blanket, and rest our heads together
Upon pillows of soft hay.

Let us relax after the day's toil, and listen
To the provoking murmur of the brook.
--Kahlil Gibran

So she took her love
For to gaze awhile
Upon the fields of barley.
In his arms she fell as her hair came down
Among the fields of gold.

Will you stay with me, will you be my love,
Among the fields of barley.
We'll forget the sun in his jealous sky
As we lie in fields of gold.
--Sting, Gordon Sumner, Dusan Bogdanovic

"Brian, would you be open to a call in Eastern North Dakota?" It was Nelson Preus, Bishop of my home synod, on the phone.

My heart raced with excitement. Before I could respond, he continued, "So, what are you doing right now as you await a call?"

"Well," my mind spinning, but knowing I was raised to speak the truth to my superiors at all times, "I'm a host at a restaurant and I am also bartending at a country club, so that I can get free golf."

There was a awkward pause, and then Bishop Preus continued. "I received a phone call from Pastor Thor Rykken (yes, that is about as Norwegian as you can get) who is the Senior Pastor of a large church in West Fargo. They are looking to add two full- time Associate Pastors to their staff, with one of them focusing on youth ministry. Pastor Rykken ran into Pastor Elmo Anderson at St. Luke's Hospital the other day, and he suggested that you might be a good person for that call. Are you interested?"

"Of course I am!" I blurted out. "Tell me what the next steps would be!" Thus began one of those fascinating times in life when in a moment's time one's trajectory is changed radically.

When you graduate from seminary the Lutheran bishops of the United States gather to hold what we semi-affectionately refer to as the "draft." Each graduate prepares paperwork in which they indicate the top three synods they would prefer to go to for their first call, although there is no guarantee one will get any of those three. The bishops review these papers and then, in succession, each "drafts" a candidate for their synod. This continues until all candidates are selected.

Just like my experience finding out if I had made the freshman basketball team at Concordia, one day I raced to a bulletin board in one of the seminary buildings and there was listed the students and the synod to which each was assigned. I still remember going there and finding friends of mine who were a "clergy couple" both in tears. They had hoped for an urban setting but were assigned to South Dakota, and would end up with respective calls in the little towns of Bison and Buffalo (you can't make this stuff up).

I had been lucky enough to get my first choice, the Northwest Pacific, where I had interned. However, matters quickly turned south with that assignment.

It was May of 1977 and Pauline and I were preparing to host a graduation party for a number of our seminary friends in our apartment. The phone rang and it was the Assistant to the Bishop of the Northwest Pacific Synod. He excitedly told me he was pretty sure he had a call for me (congregations receive suggestions from the Bishop, but always have the final say). I asked him where it was, and he named a small town in the middle of the state, half way between Seattle and Spokane.

I reminded him that I had had only one firm request on my forms: that, because of Pauline's serious health problems, we needed to be located near a major medical center. I told him right then and there on the phone that I could not consider that call, which basically sealed my fate with that synod. As you can imagine, it is not wise for someone fresh out of seminary to say "no" to your bishop, no matter what the reason.

Now, most seminary graduates do not have a call when they graduate, but over the summer most end up with calls. Two of my best friends, Howard Stendahl and Jerry Houge, also did not have calls at graduation, and so the three of us spent a great deal of our time that summer playing golf together. In July Howard received a call that took him to Wisconsin and in August Jerry received a call to Wyoming. The three of us played our last round of golf, I crawled into my beat up 1969 Chevy Impala and was overcome by a feeling of loss and loneliness, wondering what would ever become of me.

At the end of August, in order to make room for incoming students, Luther Seminary forced us to move out of seminary housing, even though we had no place to go. We found a small apartment elsewhere in St. Paul, and I got the two aforementioned jobs.   As September passed with no interviews, my heart sank even further. Finally in October Bishop Preus' phone call led to an interview at Faith Lutheran Church in West Fargo, North Dakota, and they extended a Call to be an Associate Pastor there.

A few days later my good friend Howard flew into Fargo on a cold, wintery night, and the next day he and Pauline and I drove through a blizzard to my home congregation, North Viking Lutheran Church in Maddock, North Dakota, to be ordained on November 11, 1977.

The congregation was packed as brother Neil read the Gospel, Pauline read a statement about ordination, Howard preached and Pastor Elmo ordained me, surrounded by several classmates, including the clergy couple who were in their new calls in Buffalo and Bison, South Dakota.

After the ordination part of the service, which included the laying on of hands by family and the other pastors gathered there, it was time for me to give my response. Sitting before me were Ansel and Dorothy, my baptismal sponsors, my brothers, Pauline, her parents, members of the four families who had offered to take Alan and me into their homes after our parents died and this community of witnesses who had helped raise me for eighteen years.

I expressed my sadness that my parents, Edrei and Ruth Erickson, were not there. Then I gave thanks for the grace and love showered on me over the years from the people gathered there, and I turned to Pauline and said, "I never really understood what grace was until you chose to love me."

I was overwhelmed by all the people who attended, including friends whom I had not seen for years, such as childhood friend Billy Gorrie.

However, that would be the last time I would see Billy. Billy's dad had died in a boating accident in Canada in 1973, his mother would die in 1999, and Billy committed suicide in 2011, writing his own obituary, which was published in the Winnipeg Free Press.

As I have said before, there are two kinds of grief. One,

with which we are the most familiar, is when we lose something or someone precious to us. The other is the grief we experience regarding what we wanted and never experienced, such as being married, having children, being successful in a certain career. It also includes relationships lost in time and space. I grieve that I did not find a way to stay in touch with Billy so that I could have stood by him in his struggles.

As I settled into my new role, West Fargo turned out to be a perfect place for Pauline and me. I have discovered over the years that sometimes it is easier to start something from scratch than to incorporate your vision into a program that already exists. The youth program at Faith presented that opportunity, as there had been next to no program before I arrived. That does not mean creating such a program is easy, but it was exhilarating to have Pastor Thor put his confidence in me and allow me to create the program I thought best. He also allowed me to fully function as a pastor in all areas of parish ministry, from preaching and teaching to pastoral care and social ministry. I also did my fair share of baptisms, weddings and funerals.

I shall never forget my first funeral. The elderly father of a family tangentially related to the congregation died in Jamestown, North Dakota, and they asked to have the funeral at Faith. I had never met the man to be buried, which has been true of probably half the funerals I have officiated over the years.

I pulled out my seminary notes and sat down with the family to plan the service. When it came to music they wanted a couple of John Philip Sousa marches. I gently tried to direct them towards some of the great hymns of our tradition, to which the family firmly objected: "He was not very religious, but he was patriotic." At that point I put my clergy foot down and said there shall be at least one hymn. I provided a few suggestions and they reluctantly picked one, probably Amazing Grace, which is not my favorite but is clearly the cultural favorite of North Americans when they decide to venture into the spiritual realm.

The day came for the funeral and about fifteen people showed up, all of them family. I led the service with great grace and dignity, and when it was over, they stood up and marched out of the sanctuary, not saying a word to me. Welcome to parish ministry!

Pastor Thor was a great supervising pastor. Not only did he give me total freedom to develop the youth program, but also I was treated as co-equal in all aspects of parish ministry. Faith was a very supportive and affirming congregation, and I soon found myself enjoying most aspects of parish ministry. And, situated a block from the high school in a growing community, there was no lack of youth with which to work.

Although many youth pastors and directors focus on junior high youth, I decided to concentrate on high school youth, which, in West Fargo, was a four-year program, beginning in 9th grade. I still remember our very first event. Pauline and I decided a hospitable start might be to invite all the high school youth to our apartment. Two youth showed up. This was not a rousing success, but it was, like the biblical mustard seed, a tiny seed that would grow into a large bush. Those two youth became key leaders, and within four years I would lead a three-day winter retreat at my old Bible camp, Red Willow, that had a turn-out of 60 high school youth.

Faith was also a great situation for Pauline. She not only assisted me with the youth program, but she taught the high school Sunday School class. She also helped me develop a weekend marriage retreat that she and I led with the other Associate Pastor and his wife.

Pauline's neurological condition had improved to the point that she could drive a car again (you had to be seizure-free for six months in order to maintain a driver's license). She was able to read well enough that she decided to return to school to study social work.

Out of Pauline's own experiences of suffering grew deep compassion for others who suffered. She took courses focusing on the struggles of Native Americans and other minority cultures, women, the elderly, and those with various physical disabilities.

She carried this learning over into her work with high school youth. One evening she had me rent two wheelchairs and she assigned two youth to be the ones using the chairs, and the others were given the task of assisting them. They then went as a group out to dinner and afterwards processed what that experience had been like, both for the ones "disabled," and for those assisting them.

In one of her school papers Pauline argued that oppression happens when people self-centeredly conform to the culture and world around them, and that, instead, "there are times when we should be different, when it is called for and needed. We should be upset and rebel against world hunger and starvation; we should demand justice for all and equality for all. We should strive for love and concern in all our friendships."

Pauline also took courses on death, dying, bereavement and suicide, and in a paper described her concern: "I faced [my own death], however much on the surface, eight years ago. I was told in all probability I would suffer a premature death. Foremost in my mind has been the fear of my husband's death."

In the spring of 1978 Pauline volunteered as a counselor at the Juvenile Detention Center in Moorhead. She loved her work, and by summer she was hired to work there on a part-time basis, which she would do for the next two years as she continued her studies.

For me, theologically, I continued to try to find ways of using the hope-filled teaching of the theology of hope in my preaching and teaching. I soon learned that preaching really is an art form, which, in part, means finding ways to proclaim or teach something without directly saying what you are doing. I

didn't say, "Now I am going to talk about the theology of hope." Instead I tried to find examples of hope in our daily struggles. I didn't say, "Now I am going to talk about Luther's theology of the cross." Instead I tried to tell stories of how God is with us in the pain and suffering of life. I didn't say, "Now, as Karl Marx or Sigmund Freud wrote," but I talked about the alienation so often present in our work situations and in our families of origin.

It's interesting. Several years after I had left one of the congregations in which I served, I received a Christmas card from one of the members who told me that she missed my sermons about hope. It had never occurred to me that someone might summarize my sermons in that way, but I found the comment to be affirming of what—if I were to sit down and describe it—I wanted people to experience in my preaching. After all, as St. Paul puts it, faith, hope and love are what abide, and, at many times in life, hope is the most important.

There is one other area of theology on which I decided to focus, an area in which most people have a deep interest: the relationship of God to human suffering.

As I explained earlier, I was raised to believe that everything that happens, good or bad, is God's will. This theology grows out of the philosophic desire to prove God by assuming that, if there is a God, this God must be the greatest and biggest and best of all things. So God is omniscient, knowing all things ahead of time. God is omnipresent, able to be at all places at all times. God is omnipotent, having power over all things. Throw all this together, and you come up with a portrait of a God who knows everything that is going to happen, is in charge of everything that happens and can be everywhere at the same time to make sure those things happen.

This is far more a Greek view of God than a Hebrew one, and really does not coincide well with what we discover in scripture. And, as I had already experienced, this view of God can lead to anger at God for deciding when and where and how we suffer.

As I became more comfortable in parish ministry and felt closer to God again, I decided to tackle this theological issue head on. One of the reasons for this was that, if Pauline were to die, I did not want to experience the same kind of separation from God I felt after my parents died.

I decided to head back to Luther Seminary for a continuing education seminar on this very subject, with one of the speakers being one of the brightest and most profound professors at Luther, Dr. Paul Sponheim. Working from what is called Process Theology, he classified evil in three main categories. The first is natural evil, such as earthquakes and floods. The second is moral evil, caused by human sin, such as holocausts and genocides. The third, which is the most obtuse, is metaphysical evil, which is part of the structure of reality as created by God. We may not think of it as evil, but mortality, for instance, means we will die, and being finite means we are limited in our power to do good, both of which may come to us as forms of suffering.

Now, of course, if God is indeed the creator of our present reality, then, in a sense, you can blame God for everything: Why a creation with natural evil? Why the limits on human freedom through mortality and being finite? Why create humans with a free will that allows them to do unspeakable forms of cruelty?

However, what if God is not omnipotent and omniscient. Process Theology asserts that God's love is greater than God's power, and love, as St. Paul puts it, does not insist on its own way. God, rather than controlling human behavior, gives us free will and then tries to guide us, to "woo us," to do the good and the right. However, we have the freedom to refuse to listen and to be disobedient.

Most of the great evil in the world is moral evil, caused by human beings. God does not cause mass shootings in schools. Humans choose to do that. God does not bomb people. Humans do that.

God also does not decide when someone will die. Sometimes that can be found in moral sin, as, in the case of my father, who chose to smoke most of his life. Sometimes it is just the mystery of the universe, as when a child is born with a terminal illness or gets cancer at an early age.

In Process Theology the future is not pre-determined.

Humans have a part in what happens, the good happens when we follow God and the bad happens when we rebel against God, which has been the case since Adam and Eve and Cain and Abel.

From a pastoral and spiritual point of view, this theology makes it possible to view God, not as the cause of our suffering, but as someone, demonstrated most clearly in Christ, who is with us in our suffering, crying with us.

Some people just seem to know this intuitively, as was the case with Pauline. She never blamed God for her illness, and she seemed always to feel that God was with her in her suffering.

I, on the other hand, had to take the academic route. I had to find a theology that gave me hope, and brought me closer to God rather than driving me from God.

It is one thing to come to this conclusion in the classroom or by reading a book. It is another thing to see if a theology "works" in the midst of reality. It if does work, that doesn't mean it is necessarily true, but (and this will surprise a lot of people), the church has always asserted that if something "works," that must be considered—along with other factors—as evidence of a possible truth.

For example, over the centuries as the church had to decide which books would make it into the Bible and which would not--and churches do not agree on the same list of books--one of the bases of decision was whether that book brought comfort and hope to those reading it.

It would not be long before I would have a chance to see if this new theology worked for me.

In Fargo-Moorhead Pauline and I experienced the summertime of our love. Our marriage grew more and more strong, and individually we each found increasing fulfillment in our vocational lives. Pauline relished her involvement in school and church and found great satisfaction in her work at the Juvenile Detention Center. Finally she was able to do, on a limited basis, so many of the things she had wanted to do during our early years of marriage. She had to pace herself, but she was able to be far more active than she had been.

We always made sure we had plenty of time together to converse, sharing our joys and hopes, our problems and fears. Sometimes these conversations occurred over dinner out, sometimes on short trips to visit family or friends. We also ended nearly every day by sitting in our living room, sipping wine, and talking. Through those countless hours of sharing, we grew in our understanding of each other and ourselves, and our love deepened.

However, summer would not last. Pauline's disease would not lie dormant. The progression began at Thanksgiving, 1979. Pauline developed a severe cold. It was the first of many colds that winter, several of which developed into bronchitis, as her lungs continued to deteriorate.

Pauline began to retain more and more fluids as her heart weakened. Her stomach and ankles became quite enlarged. Her doctor placed her on diuretics and prescribed a new drug, Isuprel, which greatly improved her lung capacity. The primary use of this drug is to speed up the heart, but one of the side effects is to dilate the arteries of the lungs.

In Pauline's case the positive effects from this dilation of the arteries, which made it easier for her blood to flow, actually slowed the speed of her heart. Her breathing became less labored, often to a level that surprised even her doctors.

One evening that spring, shortly after Pauline began taking Isuprel, we walked over to a neighbor's house just a block away. On the way home Pauline literally "took off." I couldn't believe it! All those years I had had to walk slowly so that Pauline could keep up with me. That evening I had trouble keeping up with her! We were elated! Finally something was available, medically, that helped her condition.

Our excitement and optimism would not last long. Pauline and I took a vacation in June at Riding Mountain, Canada to relax, read and to play a round of golf on a gorgeous course that Ansel and Dad had once played.

We headed to Canada and were having a beautiful, relaxing time, but I noticed that Pauline seemed to be getting more winded as she walked. By the end of the week her stomach became extremely bloated, and she had difficulty breathing.

We returned home early and her doctor increased her intake of diuretics and recommended bed rest. A week later there was still no improvement, and Pauline had retained approximately thirty pounds of excess fluids.

On July 7 her doctor admitted her to Dakota Hospital. A lung scan showed that she had almost total blockage of blood flow to the left lung. She was put on oxygen and blood thinners.

By the next morning she was still getting worse, with her pulse up and her breathing labored. She was moved into intensive care, and her doctor asked to meet with Pauline's parents and me. He explained her condition and what they were trying to do for her, and then Pauline's father asked if it would be a good idea to call Pauline's sisters. His response slammed reality into my face: "Yes, that might be a good idea, in case she doesn't survive."

I had one of those out of body experiences where you feel like you are in a nightmare, wondering if this is really happening. I couldn't believe it! But I had to believe it! All the denial I had harbored those past few days, indeed, for several years, was now shattered.

I asked to see Pauline, and the next day I began journaling, my first entry recounting that visit:

> What could I say to someone who had already suffered so much? I had to let her know this was serious, that she had to fight, and yet I didn't want to scare her and put any more stress on her already failing heart.
>
> Pauline opened her eyes and looked up at me. Her eyes pleaded with me as she whispered softly, "I want to go home."
>
> "Honey," I replied, "this is serious." Quietly tears began to stream down her cheeks. I thought my heart would break in two.

I was flooded with emotions, including fear, anger and guilt. Guilt that I had allowed her to stay home so long before taking her to the hospital. Anger at her doctors for not admitting her sooner.

I struggled with how much to tell Pauline about her condition, and how much I should just try to be strong for her. I decided to take the latter course, and not put any more stress on her when she was in such a weakened state, thinking she had to take care of me.

I also vowed never to let her go to the doctor alone again. Normally, she wanted me to wait in the lobby while she had her appointments. However, that is a risky thing to do. When you are the patient, you want so badly to be well that you tend to hear only the positive comments from the doctor. Your spouse or loved-one hears exactly the opposite. You pick up on anything negative, and are much more likely to press the doctor for an exact prognosis.

Five days before Pauline was admitted to the hospital, her doctor—I found out later—had given her a choice: she could stay at home if she stayed in bed, or she could be admitted, receive oxygen and have further tests administered if her condition didn't improve.

Pauline, of course, wanted to be at home, and took that option. I knew that if I had been with her I would have pushed for her being admitted right then. She could have had oxygen, the lung scan could have been done sooner and the blood thinners administered earlier. Now it might be too late!

Pauline hovered near death Wednesday, Thursday and Friday. I slept in the ICU family room and went in to see her whenever I was allowed. I held her hand, encouraged her to be positive and tried to help her sleep and rest. She loved to have me tell her stories. That helped her relax and sleep. I had never thought of myself as that kind of a storyteller, but I did the best I could.

We brought in another doctor for a second opinion, but he simply confirmed what our doctor had told us. However, he related facts that I did not know, facts that filled me with deep fear. The average life expectancy once this disease is diagnosed is five years. Pauline had already survived ten years. He told us that her condition was very serious, there was no other treatment to be tried and that she might very well die.

With Pauline I continued to emphasize the positive. I told her how much I loved her, how happy she had made me, how much I needed her and encouraged her to relax, rest and trust that she would get better. And, whenever I would leave her room, I would say to her: "Honey, I love you with all my heart. Always have. Always will!"

I asked Pauline's doctor what the symptoms would be if she started to get even worse. He said her fever would rise, her blood pressure would fall and her pulse would not come down. Hour after hour I watched the heart monitor, my eyes glued to those digital numbers indicating her pulse rate. A digital number, which showed me whether the heart I loved so fervently was moving towards death or life.

When I was out of Pauline's room I spent much of my time in prayer, either in the hospital chapel or across the street under a large cross outside a Catholic Church

For the first five days Pauline was in the hospital her condition remained about the same. Finally, on Saturday, I decided to go home to take a shower. While at home I got a call from the hospital. Pauline wanted me. I asked the nurse about Pauline's condition, and she confirmed my worst fears: her fever was up and her blood pressure was down.

I raced to the hospital and went into Pauline's room. I held her hand, and she went to sleep. She slept for two hours. I kept holding her hand and prayed and prayed.

Finally she woke up. She looked at me, smiled, and whispered: "Don't worry. I'll be okay." Then the nurse came in. Pauline's fever had broken and her blood pressure was up.

That was the turning point. Her condition was still serious, but slowly she began to improve. She was in the ICU a total of eight days, and then spent 21 more days in a private room.

The day she was moved to that private room, I was

filled with relief and joy. Not only was Pauline improving, but now we could have some privacy, and I could sleep in the reclining chair right beside her bed, which I did every night. Finally, early in August, I was able to bring her home.

Pauline's activities had to be severely limited. She was on oxygen 16-20 hours a day. At first, about all she could do was walk to the bathroom. She spent long hours sleeping, and was able to do some reading and visiting. Slowly she improved, but she could no longer walk stairs or more than a couple of blocks.

She had to quit her job, and she was not allowed to drive because of the seizures she had in the hospital. Once again Pauline suffered severe losses, and she grieved these changes. But she was alive, we were together and we rejoiced in that. Each moment, each day, was more precious than ever.

Early in September classes resumed at Moorhead State. I tried to assert my role as "protector," but Pauline would have none of it. Either I would take her to school or she would find her own way. The only compromise I could get out of her was a promise to take her portable oxygen tank with her to class. She reluctantly agreed, but never used it in class. She wanted to appear as normal as she possibly could, even if that meant some physical discomfort.

Late in September Pauline would experience another loss. Her cat had been hit by a car and was dead. I found a box, laid Freddy in it, and brought him into the garage. There was Pauline. She had taken off her oxygen and come outside.

Tears came to Pauline's eyes as she bent over Freddy, and began to pet him. Then she began to shake him over and over again, "Wake up, Freddy! Please wake up! Please wake up!" Tears also came to my eyes. For Pauline, yes, but also for me as I tried to force out of my consciousness the image of myself doing the same.

As the leaves began to fall, we recaptured the summer of our love. Pauline slowly developed more strength. She enjoyed school and resumed teaching her high school church class, now hosting it on Wednesday nights in our home. The discussions in those classes were deeper than ever. Pauline had a gift for creating an atmosphere with youth that encouraged free and open discussion. On those evenings she and her class dealt with issues like discrimination, death, funeral practices, sexism and racism.

Pauline struggled with the purpose of her life and what lay ahead for her. Her doctor had been quite vague regarding her new prognosis. He was concerned not to paint too bleak a future for her, fearing she might become too depressed. However, I had talked to him alone several times in the hospital and I knew the grim prognosis.

Again I struggled with how much I should tell Pauline. I had always operated previously with the theory that the patient has the right to know everything, and in most cases should. But it seemed different now when it was the life of Pauline that was in question.

Pauline, however, wanted to know. She pressed her doctor, and she pressed me. Step by step I would tell her what I knew. She was not surprised by what she heard. Her weakened body was telling her much the same.

In November Pauline's doctor told her she would probably get no better than she was then. She could not walk stairs, she was weak and tired easily and she was still on oxygen all night and most of the day. With this news Pauline began to grieve anew all she had lost. She struggled with what the future held for her, writing in her journal on December 2, 1980:

> I always had felt self-pity was a despicable feeling— but not any more. True, to be healthy we cannot linger with that feeling. But every one of us has in our lifetime come face-to-face with self-pity. For some it is extremely transient. For others it overstays it's welcome. But for some self-pity is an honorable step toward becoming a total person.
>
> I want to say, God, where are you? But I know you're here with me and that you care. But I hurt. I need you

and you're here—but I still hurt. Shouldn't your presence comfort me more than it does? What am I lacking? Perhaps I have to fully work through my grief before the comfort.

A week later she wrote to her best friend, Mary, explaining that her doctor had told her that she would not improve further, concluding:

My life expectancy is low—I'm "forgetting" the numbers he quoted me, for I have already beaten the odds. Bear and I cried, went through (and still are) bereavement and we feel closer than ever. I don't know what I'd do without him!

My plans for the future have to be quite minimal. As for now, I'm planning on getting my degree, then hopefully working part-time or doing volunteer work.

As winter wore on it became clear to us that we should attempt to move to a warmer climate. Not only was it extremely difficult for Pauline to walk in the cold air, but also the flu and cold season were dangerous to her with her deteriorated lungs.

In January I went to Bishop Preus and asked if he would contact the Bishop of the Southern California Synod regarding a possible call to a church there, and he set the process in motion.

On January 21, 1981, Pauline wrote:

Dear God, Thank you! No, not for death, nor my human condition, even though fundamentalists say I "should." I'm ill—it's a dirty shame—but something you certainly did not cause and I feel it would be blasphemy for me to thank you for "it."

But thank you for giving me the tools to see to see my life beyond my illness, in spite of my illness, and the ability to love life even though I am unhealthy and perhaps may die in the not-so-distant future. Granted, I still get jealous of healthy, productive people—but not despairingly so, for there are things in my life I feel blessed to have.

> Mainly Bear. Because of Bear I can honestly say I'm a fulfilled, joyful, loving person. No matter how debilitating my illness makes me, I will have Bear to love, hold and cry with. Bear makes it possible for me to reach out and help others more unfortunate than myself, and that includes the whole human race. I feel like the luckiest person alive!

In March we received a phone call that finally gave us some hope in the midst of all the depressing events. Her sister, Carole, who now lived in California near Stanford University Medical Center, called to inform us that a heart-lung transplant had been performed at Stanford on a woman who had the exact disease that Pauline had.

From that day forward Pauline set her heart and mind on having such a transplant when her conditioned worsened, and now it made even more sense for me to try to get a call to California so doctors at Stanford could monitor her condition.

We welcomed the coming warmth and sunshine of spring, and Pauline began to do volunteer work at a nursing home in Fargo.

However, it soon became apparent that even this volunteer work was too strenuous, which also meant she did not have the strength to do the social work internship necessary to complete her degree.

She discussed this with her advisor, who arranged for Pauline to graduate with a B.S. degree in Human Services. On May 22, 1981 Pauline graduated and I threw a surprise party for her at our house. On a beautiful, spring evening we celebrated Pauline's accomplishments and, even more so, her presence.

The reality of death intensifies life. It makes us more aware of the joy, beauty and love that are in our lives. We try to treasure those moments, because we know they are fleeting and, in spite of our best attempts at denial, temporal.

The threat of death never leaves those in love the same. Either they, out of fear, drift apart, or, out of thanksgiving, huddle together against the thunderstorms gathering in the distance. The more Pauline suffered and lost, the closer we huddled together and the deeper our love grew.

On June 29, Pauline gave me a card, in which she wrote:

> Bear, My Love, It is you and me, and together, sweetheart, we can combat anything. Sometimes we may feel alone or that we are fighting a hopeless battle. But thank God for our togetherness. I really believe God understands how much we need each other, and if she can make our lives longer together, she will. We have faith, we have hope, we have our love. And the promise of everlasting love, Pauline.

It was still the summer of our love, but summer was moving by fast. At any time we knew the leaves could begin to turn, and the ripened fruit fall to the ground. What were we facing? Death and separation? Or a transplant that would give Pauline a quality of life that she had not known for many years? What were we facing? Autumn, and then winter? Or a return to spring?

Chapter 7　Autumn

Let us go and gather the grapes of the vineyard
For the winepress, and keep the wine in old
Vases, as the spirit keeps Knowledge of the
Ages in eternal vessels.

Let us return to our dwelling, for the wind has
Caused the yellow leaves to fall and shroud the
Withering flowers that whisper elegy to Summer.
Come home, my eternal sweetheart, for the birds
Have made pilgrimage to warmth and left the chilled
Prairies suffering pangs of solitude. The jasmine
And myrtle have no more tears.

Let us retreat, for the tired brook has
Ceased its song; and the bubblesome springs
Are drained of their copious weeping; and
The cautious old hills have stored away
Their colorful garments.
Come, my beloved: Nature is justly weary
And is bidding her enthusiasm farewell
With quiet and contented melody.
  --Kahlil Gibran

Summer rushes in on the heels of spring, eager to take her
turn; and then she dances with wild abandon. But the time
soon comes when she gratefully falls, exhausted and sated,
into the auburn arms of autumn.
  — Cristen Rodgers

"I can't believe how beautiful and peaceful the lake is. I really loved our time here in Chicago." Pauline was standing at the window of our lakeside room in the Lake Shore Holiday Inn, overlooking Lake Michigan. It was early July, and we were taking a romantic trip we had long dreamed of: a return to the city where we had spent our first two years of marriage. We visited our apartment, the Lutheran School of Theology where I had started seminary and many of the places we used to frequent, including our favorite restaurants in Old Town.

The awareness of time creates a certain strangeness about life. In the present, no matter how wonderful, we dream of the future, assuming it can only be better. Then, when we arrive at the future, and return to the past, that past is often so much more beautiful than we had realized at the time. We keep telling ourselves to live in the present, and celebrate its joys, but it seems our carried anxieties always take their toll, and it is only from the perspective down the road that, looking back, we realize how wonderful the past was.

Returning to Fargo, I boarded a plane late in July to fly to Hemet, California, some 90 miles east of Los Angeles, for an interview at Trinity Lutheran Church. In August I received a call as Associate Pastor, and we began to make plans for moving in September.

We said goodbye to our many friends in Fargo-Moorhead-West Fargo and to the wonderful members of Faith Lutheran Church, who had supported us with such love during Pauline's illness and recovery, and headed west on another road trip, which we always enjoyed so much. However, as soon as we reached Wyoming the high altitude adversely affected Pauline's breathing and it did not improve until we dropped to a lower altitude in California.

I began my work at Trinity Lutheran in October, we decorated a very nice house we had rented, with lots of fruit trees in the back yard, and we began to explore the area. Autumn in the high desert felt like summer in the Midwest, which renewed our hope for the future.

Even though Pauline's health was slightly worse, we were buoyed by the fact that we now lived in a better climate for her and closer to Stanford University Medical Center. We contacted a cardiologist at the Loma Linda Medical Center nearby, Dr. Robert Marsa, and Pauline had her first examination with him in November.

Pauline desperately wanted to get involved in life in Hemet, and decided to teach the high school Sunday School class as she had done in West Fargo, hosting it in our home on Wednesday evenings, as it was no longer possible for her to attend church on Sunday mornings. If Pauline was to go out at all, it had to be later in the day when her breathing had improved from her medicines kicking in.

We also involved ourselves with a couples club of young adults at church, and these folks quickly became our good friends. My call included all aspects of parish ministry, but, as in West Fargo, my primary focus was youth ministry. There already was a fairly strong program in place, and I incorporated the emphases and programs I had developed at Faith Lutheran. I also began a motion choir (which we had in West Fargo) of youth using movement to interpret spiritual music in worship. Pauline had wanted to direct this choir herself, but realized early on that she did not have the energy for it.

Love is the source of our meaning in life, but it does not end there. We were created to reach out in love to others, and that is what Pauline wanted to do. Her increasing inability to do that frustrated her, and she kept looking for other ways to share herself.

I often found myself feeling conflicted. I wanted to fulfill my call at Trinity in a responsible and effective way, but I also worried about Pauline and wanted to be with her as much as possible, both to bring her comfort, but also to make her comfortable. Our increasingly difficult situation meant almost every day I had challenging decisions about how exactly to spend my time and energy.

There is no way around it. Sometimes, when someone you love is seriously ill, you end up running on fumes. And yet, you often don't notice it because you are so focused on their well-being and what you can do to make sure everything that can be done for them is done.

One aspect of this challenge is the creative scheduling that is often required. Previously, I had built my youth programs around overnight retreats, which I found to be much more effective and meaningful than events at church or in the community. That winter I planned an overnight retreat in the San Jacinto Mountains near Idyllwild. Now I arranged with the other adult counselors for me to be able to drive home in the evening to be with Pauline, and then to return the next morning. Fortunately for me, both Pastor Don, my pastoral partner, and the entire congregation were very understanding of my situation, and supportive as I made these kinds of adjustments to my ministry.

We had a wonderful Christmas. Pauline's parents spent several weeks with us over the holidays, staying in a guest room we had set up especially for them. Brother Alan also came for several days at Christmas.

In February,1982, we went for our second visit with Dr. Marsa. We had decided to ask him if he would contact Stanford and ask doctors there if they would be willing to monitor Pauline's condition. Before we could ask him about this possibility, Dr. Marsa addressed us, explaining that he had been wondering if Pauline would be willing to consider having a heart/lung transplant? He thought she would be an excellent candidate and had a good chance of being accepted into the program at Stanford.

We were elated! This was one of the main reasons we had moved, and now our hopes and dreams of a possible transplant were beginning to become a reality.

We also asked Dr. Marsa if he thought Pauline might improve any further. Her health had been somewhat worse since the move and we had hoped that once she got settled in to her new life that her condition might improve. Dr. Marsa said that further improvement was unlikely, and that her condition was most likely getting worse.

The more Pauline's outward activities had to be limited, the more she turned inward to find meaning in her spirituality and in our love. In February she began journaling again on a regular basis. Her entries reflect the paradoxical situation in which we found ourselves, not knowing whether we were preparing for renewed health or for death. She wrote excitedly about her hopes for the future, and yet she was realistic about the possibility of her death.

She expressed her hopes in a Valentine's card to me, writing, "I love you. Honey, you make life worth fighting for. Because of you, I am optimistic for the future. There will be a day when we will chase our dreams together, both running. Love you forever, Paul."

By now, Pauline had been seizure-free long enough that she could again have a driver's license, which gave her some semblance of freedom.

In the spring Trinity had decided to begin a new program that trained laypeople to do hospital and homebound visitation, and to support those in grief. Pauline decided to sign up for the weekly sessions, driving herself to the classes.

On an evening in early March, when Pauline had gone to a session of this class, I was at home watching television when I heard a horn honking in the driveway. I looked out the window and saw our car, Pauline slumped over the steering wheel, having difficulty catching her breath.

I ran outside, rolling a large oxygen tank. I put the cannula into her nose and carried Pauline into the house, rolling the tank at the same time. When she felt better, she told me what had happened.

Pauline's seizures were caused primarily by shortness of breath and hyperventilating. As a result, not enough oxygen would reach her brain and she would pass out, going into an epileptic-type seizure.

That evening, at the mid-point in the class, her breathing became labored. As usual, she had left her oxygen in the car, as she did not like to use it in public, not wanting people to feel sorry for her. She took an Isuprel, waited for it to work, and then decided she better go to the car for the oxygen. About halfway there she realized she was in trouble, but decided to continue toward the car. The next thing she knew she found herself laying face down in the parking lot, coming out of a seizure. Her breathing labored, she had managed to crawl into the car, rest for a while and then drive the short distance home.

I was filled with fear and anguish. Not only because seizures were very hard on her heart, but also because she was on blood thinners to keep her lungs from clotting, which meant that any kind of gash or cut could have led to severe bleeding.

The signs were becoming unmistakable, no matter how much we wanted to repress the truth. Pauline was getting worse, her condition clearly deteriorating. This was confirmed on our next appointment with Dr. Marsa. We asked if he had heard anything from Stanford. He had not, but promised to call there the next morning.

The following day Pauline picked up her journal and wrote:

> I look around at this world and feel sad—sad because I am not "intensely aware" of my life and the beauty of it. I've read that when one faces death, one becomes radiantly alive. Something is wrong here . . . With all the things going on in this world, all the things needing to be done, all the people suffering, I "should" be focusing on something besides TV.
>
> I do want to leave something to this world, but I have so little energy. And most of the energy I have to spare is directed to Bear. I love him; I'm going to miss him; I want to be with him every waking moment until I die. Yes, I can hear the birds chirping and smell the flowers. It's wonderful to be alive!

As Pauline's condition worsened, and she had to increasingly restrict her activities, we began to take drives in our car together. She really loved to get out for a while, breathe the fresh air and look around the beautiful valley in which we lived.

One of our favorite drives was into the hills south of Hemet. From there we could look down on the city and the valley, and, in the evening, at the sparkling lights below us. How peaceful, how serene, how good it was to be alive, to be together. We talked openly about both our hopes and our fears, and found comfort in sharing those feelings honestly with each other.

As word began to spread about Pauline's worsening condition, our friends in the church sprang into action, and began bringing meals over. Pauline enjoyed not only the fact that I didn't have to shop and cook, but that she had a chance to visit with these amazingly loving and caring friends. On March 13 she wrote:

> Dear God, please help me to live long enough so I can help and touch more people's lives. I am your servant. Please help me to truly relinquish all foolish claims to be in control of my life! I want my life to mean something, and it only can when I is i, and i let you be rightfully in charge. (Pauline purposely used the small i to refer to herself.)

Pauline's breathing now was continually labored, which not only meant she had to stay at home more, but it also restricted her movement around the house. As she sat in a chair in the living room, she wrote:

> I am sitting in the living room, not much more than sixteen feet from the dining room. That's where I would like to be. I could listen to music, have good light and a hard surface to write upon. But no o o o o o (John Belushi, you left your mark!) Sixteen feet for me now is like six blocks, or more. It would take so much energy to get there—is it worth it? What, really, is worth my scarce supply of energy?

It was that week that we finally received some good news. Dr. Marsa called and informed us that Stanford was interested in interviewing Pauline as a possible candidate for heart-lung transplantation. An appointment at Stanford was set for early April. Before that, we drove to Loma Linda University Hospital for two interviews with a social worker who had been asked by Stanford to assess Pauline's character as a possible transplant recipient.

The social worker wanted to know about Pauline and me: our families, our relationship, our religious convictions. All factors surrounding the recipient of a transplant are important. Did Pauline have the will to survive? Was she a fighter? What reasons did she have for wanting to extend her life? How strongly would her family and I support her? How did her religious convictions fit in with such a radical surgery?

The social worker was caring, sensitive and gentle. All in all it was a positive experience for both of us. But how strange it seemed to be interviewed, not for school, not for a job—but for a surgery that could mean the difference between life and death; a surgery which would be predicated upon one person's death for another person's life.

And then there was the issue of money. Pauline was on Medicare for disability, but it probably would not cover the surgery because the government would likely consider it to be "experimental." We hoped that my insurance plan would cover the surgery, which my insurance manual indicated it would. But what if I had interpreted it incorrectly? After a nervous weekend waiting for Monday to arrive, I called my insurance company and received the good news that they would cover us. Finally, finally, the picture was beginning to brighten. There was still plenty of uncertainty, plenty of fears, but now at least there appeared to be a chance for a successful surgery. There seemed to be a stronger basis for hope.

We began preparations for our trip to Stanford for the final interview, and in her journal Pauline wrote early in April:

> When I become seriously ill, will I continually be
> depressed because my little mental game can no

longer bolster me? After a bit of trepidation, I can answer a hopeful no. I do not think my positive attitude will desert me—off and on, perhaps, but never completely. For I have my belief and faith in God, who gives me courage and, more importantly, love. I have Bear. Our love is everlasting. I have the love of my family. The love of my friends. I am truly blessed. I have been to the mountaintop. Life is beautiful: it hurts, but I can leave it.

On Palm Sunday Pauline and I tape-recorded a conversation. She talked about her surgery:

If I die, I want to die on the table. I want to give my life a chance. I really don't think I'm going to die. But if I do, I've had 31 beautiful years. I love you with all my heart. I always have and I always will. And perhaps I'll say that from a hospital bed again. But, honey, I'm going to pull through, hopefully. And, if I don't, it's not God's will, and it's not me.

Then, speaking of Christ's passion, she said, "What else can give us more feeling, more strength, than to know that he suffered for us?"

The next day I loaded up the car with oxygen tanks, wheelchair and suitcases, and Pauline and I headed for Palo Alto. At Stanford the pulmonary specialist explained that so far they had performed six heart-lung transplants, and four of the recipients had survived. Two other persons were on the waiting list, presently residing near Stanford, ready for surgery once matching donor organs became available. Stanford already had had over 300 requests for the surgery, and had been experiencing a great shortage of donor organs.

Pauline and I both felt somewhat devastated. The situation looked bleak. The odds of being accepted into the program seemed so slim.

Then we met the transplant surgeon, Dr. Stuart Jamieson. He strode into the room in green surgical garb, wearing cowboy boots, and once he spoke, we knew he was from England.

This gentle, sensitive man asked few questions. He simply told Pauline that she would make an excellent candidate. He also spoke of the shortage of donor organs and the difficulty of making a clear prognosis regarding the progression of her disease. However, he also talked about the tremendous difference the surgery can make, giving a new lease on life and greatly increasing what one is able to do.

In the same morning our hopes had been almost crushed, and then resurrected. That night, now on our way back home to Hemet, we talked over everything we had heard, focusing, of course, on whether Pauline would be accepted into the program. Pauline was more positive than me. From the beginning she felt a deep trust in Dr. Jamieson, and she was buoyed by his positive comments about her qualities as a candidate.

On Saturday night--as I had to get up sooner on Sunday than usual for the youth Easter breakfast—we began to get ready for bed early. By the time I got to bed I found Pauline on the edge of our bed, hyperventilating. I turned up her oxygen, laid her down and gave her a small, paper bag into which to breathe. I was too late; another seizure claimed her weakened body.

It was becoming starkly clear that Pauline could handle little physical exertion. And her seizures were becoming even more fearsome to me. Not only because of the headaches she would have to endure for a day or two, but also because of the pressure they put on her weakening heart.

During each seizure there was a period of time when Pauline's jaw would lock and she would quit breathing and turn blue. This put tremendous stress on her heart. I had begun, during these seizures, to listen to her heart. In the middle of the seizure—as she lay unconscious, not breathing—her heartbeat would slow way down. Then, as she began to recover, and needed more oxygen, her heart would speed up and begin to race. Sometimes, as Pauline would start to regain consciousness, she could not catch her breath.

She would go into a second seizure, and once she had three seizures in a row.

Early on that Easter morning I experienced the painful struggle we all go through when our work responsibilities conflict with personal issues going on in our lives. I wanted to simply stay by Pauline's side, but work beckoned, and this was, after all, Easter morning, one of the most important festivals in the church year.

As I headed off for the Easter breakfast, I woke Pauline, asking her to promise not to get out of bed until I was at home. Between our two worship services I went home and still found her asleep.

After the final worship service I raced home and found Pauline sitting up in bed. She was smiling, and wished me a happy Easter. She told me she had walked from the bed to the television on the dresser to turn it on and listen to a worship service. Then I noticed her journal lying open on the bed. She had made an entry that morning. I picked up the journal and began to read:

> Happy Easter. This Sunday is such a day of jubilation—Christ lives! In the mode of the sermon I heard today, this weekend is a microcosm of life. Friday—despair, desolation, heartbreak, hell, and death; Saturday—loneliness, grief; Sunday—joy, happiness and life anew!

> Bear, if you must face my death, remember Friday. It will be hell. But Saturday, you will be able to live through. It will be hard, but because of God's love you can do it. (In fact, you wouldn't be feeling this way without God. I truly believe our undying love for one another stems from God. In the past this has frightened me. It has seemed "too much" to be purely mortal. I've even felt guilty, thinking I love you more than God. But that's impossible. I am able to love so deeply because of my faith in God and love for her. And vice versa. We have something so

> special. I hope it lasts much longer, but, if not, we
> have had ten beautiful years.)
>
> Sunday, Bear you will be happy. You will always
> miss me, but that does not mean missing out on life.
> You're very talented. I'm sure you will do great
> things in whatever area of concern you decide upon.
> And the woman you choose to be your second wife
> will be a very lucky woman indeed. We've talked a
> lot vocationally: about marriage, there is nothing I
> want to say, except one thing. I hope you will be
> very, very happy. You, sweetheart, deserve it.

By now the tears were streaming down my face. I lay down Pauline's journal, placed my head in her lap, and began to sob uncontrollably. Then the words poured out of me: "Pauline, are you going to die? Pauline, are you going to leave me?"

When her condition had not improved by Tuesday morning, I called Dr. Marsa and he told me to bring her to the hospital immediately There was little now that the doctors could do for her. A transplant was her only hope.

A few days later, now back at home, Pauline wrote in her journal, reflecting on her condition and how best to use her limited energy:

> The last two weeks have been hectic, and life
> changing. It was great traveling up to Stanford with
> Bear, even with oxygen tanks and wheelchair. It
> was a bit of our old life together—traveling, seeing
> new country and settling in for fun nights in motels.
>
> The doctors at Stanford were quite optimistic about
> me as a candidate, which made us very happy.
> However, I do absolutely nothing. Bear wheels me
> from room to room, I use a commode and I get
> exhausted reading!

158

> I want to get a tan, see my friends, etc., but I am lying low. You might say I am gambling—betting that I will have the surgery and survive. If not, I don't know how worthwhile these last few months of my life will be.

> I pray to God I do not become too demanding. I want to make things as easy as possible for Bear.

Demanding was the last thing that Pauline was. At the end of our evenings, before going to bed together, I would roll her into the bathroom so she could wash her face, brush her teeth and go to the bathroom before going to bed. I would leave her there and start getting ready for bed myself.

When Pauline was done, she seldom called out to me. She just waited for me to return on my own timeline, no matter how long that was. Often when I would return, I would find her sitting quietly in her wheelchair, ready for bed, staring off into the distance, refusing to call me.

Later that week Pauline wrote to a friend in North Dakota, sharing the details of her visit to Stanford, including the large number of people wanting transplants and the shortage of donors. She ended her letter:

> I am concentrating on hanging in there for the surgery. The thought that I again will be able to run, work, etc., if everything goes okay, is so exciting. On the other hand, I can accept my death. I don't like it and will fight, but Bear and I are spending much time together. He works at home whenever possible. Between us our life is top quality because we're both here, together.

Early the next week Pauline continued writing: "Dear God, I do not want to die. Please help me hang in there until (and after) the surgery. I adamantly believe in your power to heal people. If it's your will, please heal me. God, don't take me from Bear, not yet."

After Pauline's hospital stay, I wrote to the doctors at Stanford to explain the changes in Pauline's condition. Dr. Jamieson was out of town, but as soon as he returned and found my letter, he called to inform us that Pauline would be accepted into the transplant program.

Our spirits rose and our hearts rejoiced, and that evening Pauline wrote in her journal:

> I received a call from Stu Jamieson (I love how he doesn't use his title) from Stanford today. He called in regards to our letter—I am definitely a candidate, and am after the two people now in Palo Alto. From the way Jamieson talked, I will be moved up there in a couple of months. Exciting news, but a little trepidation rears.
>
> We have so many decisions—about the house, cats, Bear's work. God, please give us the intelligence and heart to dwell upon only that which is necessary and uplifting—our being together.

The next day we began to record what we named our 10th Anniversary Tape, which was coming up on May 6. We began picking our favorite songs from our albums and recording them. As we worked on this project, Pauline wrote in her journal:

> We are beginning our tape of our life together—in celebration of our 10th Anniversary next week. The music brings back so many memories, which, thank God, are all beautiful. We have truly been blessed in our life together—our love knows no bounds.
>
> Am I dying? Yes, I feel it. Also the aloneness (of my own doing), except for Bear. I want to be by myself and meditate. Bear gave me an excellent book by Meister Eckhart, a thirteenth century Christian mystic. It has made me feel oh so inadequate, but I

feel I am getting deeper in my soul and becoming more in tune with God. This is what I need at a time like this.

I hope I will thank, either verbally or by letter, the wonderfully caring, supportive and love-filled friends I have here. I want them to know how much I appreciate their concerns, but right now I have to focus more on my inner life and peace.

Also, my energy must be saved for Bear. I feel a need to express to him my undying love, but "creative marriage" [the marriage retreat we had helped lead] isn't helping me find a new approach. All I have at my disposal are words, and I have always been verbally inadequate. I feel secure in the knowledge that it has been elucidated by me and vice versa, but I want to do something now with this dying heart.

The social worker at Stanford, Mary Burge, had given us several articles on heart-lung transplantation. Now that Pauline was officially accepted into the program, we decided to study these articles more thoroughly. That reading is reflected in Pauline's next journal entry, on May 4:

I am really afraid. All my bluster about "knowing" I'd survive the transplant, getting a job, maybe adopting children. Well, I don't know anything, and I'm scared.

When I talk to my parents and friends, I'm so strong. I'm weak only with Bear, and I don't let that happen much. Is it good for me to be optimistic or am I denying my dying? No, I do not believe I am in denial. However, for the sake of my sanity I repress my immediate future. I want to be strong when I go into surgery. One thing though: I'm going to be more honest when talking to my family and friends. I think I have this insane desire to impress everyone with my strength. No more! I'm telling it like it is.

Reading the articles on the transplant gets me down. I'll never be normal. I won't be able to get a job—tremendous job discrimination. Adoption is out—if I live six months it's considered a success (yes, six months is better than four; it is just that I had higher hopes, I guess).

Bear and I have had a unique life until now. Why should it be different after transplantation? God is with us now, and will be then if we're blessed enough to have a longer life together. I'm not going to worry, just take good care of myself so I can hang in there."

About death—am I readying for it? Should I be? I'm so glad Bear gave me Eckhart's book—I do want to go with a deeper spirituality. And I want to be with Bear. I've toyed with the idea of a more printable journal, or short stories about dying, but realize now it's just ego and the want of immortality. I've felt guilty watching TV, and reading an occasional novel: like somehow, since these very possibly are my last days, I should say, write, and think pregnantly meaningful thoughts. Nope, and no more guilt. I am happy with God and Bear.

Two days later it was our 10th wedding anniversary. I worked until 2:00 p.m. and then went home. I helped Pauline take a bath. After she rested for a while I took her outside in her wheelchair and rolled her into the backyard by the large rose bushes that were now in full bloom. She had on a red and white stripped dress. She looked gorgeous against the backdrop of the red roses. I got out our camera, put on the telephoto lens, and shot a roll of 24 portraits.

After taking Pauline back into our home I headed out to buy Chinese food. We had dinner, I opened a bottle of champagne and we began to listen to our anniversary tape, laughing and reminiscing.

I felt such joy in celebrating our life and love together, and yet I could not contain my fear about the future. At one point I commented that I hoped this was not our last anniversary celebration together. Pauline became stern, and told me to quit talking that way. Why waste this beautiful time together worried about the future? She, of course, was right.

At the end of nearly three hours of music, Pauline and I had each dedicated a song to the other. First came the song I had dedicated to her, written by Lionel Ritchie and performed by the Commodores, "Three Times a Lady."

Thanks for the times that you've given me,
The memories are all in my mind.
And now that we've come to the end of our rainbow
There's something I must say out loud!

You're once, twice, three times a lady
And I love you.
You're once, twice, three times a lady
And I love you.

You shared my dreams, my joys, my pains
You made my life worth living for
And if I had to live my life over again
I'd spend each and every moment with you

When we are together the moments I cherish,
With every beat of my heart
To touch you, to hold you, to feel you, to need you
There's nothing to keep us apart

You're once, twice, three times a lady

And I love you.
You're once, twice, three times a lady
And I love you. [Lionel Ritchie]

Then came Pauline's song dedicated to me, "If I Sing You a Love Song," performed by Bonnie Tyler.

If I sing you a love song, will you always remember?
Will you hear it on lonely nights when I'm not
 around?
If I sing you a love song, will you hear it forever?
To remind you how much I care, and how I needed
 you?

Love songs last longer than lovers ever do,
So, baby, let me sing a love song for you.
Love songs don't leave you, but lovers often do,
Oh, baby I'm afraid it could happen to me and you.

If I sing you a love song, let it always be with you.
When the others have gone away, let it still be
 there.

Love songs last longer than lovers ever do,
So, baby, let me sing a love song for you.
Love songs don't leave you like lovers often do,
Oh, baby, I'm afraid it could happen to me and you."
[Ronnie James Scott and Victor William Batty]

In the following days it became clear that Pauline was losing ground fast. In May, Dr. Jamieson told us to move to Stanford as quickly as we could. We hurriedly began to make plans to leave in a week. I had already arranged with the church leaders and Pastor Don to take a leave from work for as long as necessary for Pauline to have the transplant and recuperate.

That same day Pauline received a call from a member of the congregation whom we knew to be part of the "charismatic movement," who wanted to come over with some others to "lay hands" on Pauline and pray for healing. Pauline asked her not to come. Although we regularly prayed for such healing, she was not comfortable with was the idea that such healing could only come through a certain person who supposedly had special gifts of healing.

The next day Pauline wrote in her journal:

> Bear and I had a beautiful ten-year anniversary. We sat on the floor eating Chinese food. Later we played our tape and reminisced with the fireplace aglow, our two cats playing and candles all around. I almost felt normal. Please God, help me make it to more anniversaries with Bear!

> I am worse. Had a seizure brushing my teeth last week, so am now doing everything sitting down. We talked to Stu yesterday—are going up to Palo Alto in a week. I feel very happy to at least get this far (end of last week was very dire). However, I'm scared. This is it. I might never see this house or our cats again. Dear God, please give me courage and faith.

> Also, am I being narrow-minded not to want people whose theology I disagree with to come and pray over me? Now I feel guilty. I can say you can't come over because I'm so deathly ill, but if they called two months ago I wouldn't have wanted them—am I dogmatic, scared, or purely retaining my beliefs and feeling secure in Your arms without people touching me and telling me that.

> God, please help me. I need to feel your Grace. I guess even dying I have to feel guilt—even though I have your forgiveness. One's personality doesn't change in the throes of Death.

One evening that week we took one more ride together into the hills south of town as we had several times before. Parking in the lot of the Ramona Bowl, we looked out over the valley, sparkling with lights.

This time there were few words. Holding hands, we just stared off into the distance. We both sensed the sadness in our hearts. The fear.

Autumn was now over. What lay ahead? Spring, with its promise of new life? Or winter, and death?

The time had come. We had to move ahead. We had to leave Hemet and face the inevitable. Either Pauline would have the surgery, survive, and we would have a new life together. Or she would die.

There were no tears. Just a quiet, but firm, resolution to face the future. "God," I prayed deep in my heart, "please bring us through the valley of this disease into the brightness of a new life together."

Chapter 8   Winter

Come close to me, oh companion of my full life;
Come close to me and let not Winter's touch
Enter between us. Sit by me before the hearth,
For fire is the only fruit of Winter.

Speak to me of the glory of your heart, for
That is greater than the shrieking elements
Beyond the door.

Bind the door and seal the transoms, for the
Angry countenance of the heaven depresses my
Spirit, and the face of our snow-laden fields
Makes my soul cry.

Feed the lamp with oil and let it not dim, and
Place it by you, so I can read with tears what
Your life with me has written upon your face.
Bring Autumn's wine. Let us drink and sing the
Song of remembrance to Spring's carefree sowing,
And Summer's watchful tending, and Autumn's
Reward in harvest.

Come close to me, oh beloved of my soul; the
Fire is cooling and fleeing under the ashes.
Embrace me, for I fear loneliness; the lamp is
Dim, and the wine which we pressed is closing
Our eyes. Let us look upon each other before
They are shut.

Find me with your arms and embrace me; let
Slumber then embrace our souls as one.
Kiss me, my beloved, for Winter has stolen

All but our moving lips.

You are close by me, My Forever.
How deep and wide will be the ocean of Slumber;
And how recent was the dawn!
  --Kahlil Gibran

"O God, the strength of the weak and the comfort of sufferers: Mercifully hear our prayers and grant to your servant, Pauline, the help of your power, that her sickness may be turned into health and our sorrow into joy."

My partner in ministry, Pastor Don, was praying the closing prayers of our final worship before we headed north to Stanford. I had preached at the service, and now the congregation was uplifting us in prayer.

The moment we realize what love is, is the same moment one of life's greatest fears begins: that those we love will die.

From the moment of conception, parents worry that the new life they have created will not make it to birth. At birth parents begin a life-long journey of fearing what might happen to their child.

An infant dislikes nothing more than being left by its parents. For a growing child, nothing is more fearsome than the loss of a parent through death or divorce.

Once, when Pauline was just small girl, her father was flying to Europe on a business trip. The night before he departed she went into her parents' bedroom and said, "I sure am glad Daddy can swim, so that if the plane crashes in the sea he won't die."

Pauline actually began a kind of journal from an early age. At age thirteen she wrote: "Every night I think of what it will be like without Mom and Dad. Sweet Mom and Dad. I keep telling myself to forget it, but I can't. Dad's almost 55 and Mom's about 52. Oh, anything could happen to them. Oh please God, don't make something happen for a long, long time."

Love is always a process. It either grows or it withers. It never remains the same. The more we love, the more we fear death and separation. The irony of relationship is this: the more we find joy and meaning in love the greater our fear of losing the one we love.

Life is lived mostly on the "outside." We see the outside lives of others, including those we love. We live most of the time outside of ourselves, going through life trying so hard not to give much thought to the love and death struggle inside each of us. But it is always there, if we look for it. It is always there, controlling us consciously or unconsciously.

But for all of our attempts at repression and denial, there finally come those times when reality is slammed directly into our face. When a doctor at Dakota Hospital says, "Yes, you had better contact her sisters, in case she does not survive." When Dr. Jamieson says, "Yes, it is time to bring her to Stanford. She will not survive unless she has a transplant soon." When a congregation prays for you, asking God to turn your deathly illness into healing and new life.

Sometimes our denial is so great we forget what we ourselves have been through. To this day I will hear of someone losing a father or a mother and I will think, "Oh, that must be so difficult! How can they even handle it?" And then I remember that both of those experiences have already happened to me.

I was trying so hard not to think that Pauline could die and she was trying so hard to trust that she would have a successful transplant surgery! But now the stark reality could no longer be pushed aside and we could no longer avoid the fact that, although we prayed for new life, death was a very real possibility.

It was time to take the next step toward what awaited us. On Monday I began packing. As I did, Pauline wrote in her journal, describing her sadness and her increasing frustration at not being able to care for herself or help us prepare to move:

This might be the last time I ever see this house, see

the yard, see our trees. It's sad leaving here, but not as bad as I thought it would be. For I am scared. I want to know what my prognosis is. I'm hoping to hang in there, and I need to know for how long.

I can't stand it! Bear has been working all day and he still has a lot to do. I sit and watch. I'm full of angry impotence. I'm dirty, sweaty, and my hair is pure grease. But I cannot bother Bear. Why can't I even take care of myself?

Trickle down theory of economics. It also applies to ill people unable to care for themselves. Thank you, Bear, for not making me feel like a burden. When I do, all I have to do is tell him and he reassures me he's doing what he wants.

Our plans were to leave late Tuesday afternoon to avoid the heat, since the truck I had rented for our move did not have air conditioning. As I finished preparing for our departure Pauline wrote instructions to a friend for taking care of the plants and other items while we were gone. In the letter she wrote:

I have missed talking to you so much! However, all this reflective time has been good for me. My spiritual life has been strengthened (am now reading Christian mysticism) and I feel closer to God. Even though this has been a hard time for Bear and me, we're closer than ever. The possibility of my death makes every minute so precious to us.

I'm trying to remain positive, and am succeeding fairly well. But what's really difficult is that I must prepare for both life and death. Without surgery or divine intervention I really don't know how many months I have left.

Once again we hit the road. Pauline felt quite well, and, as usual, was in very good spirits. She knew this was her only hope, and she felt good that now she would at least have the chance for a transplant. As she had told me in April: "If I die, I want to die on the table. I want to give my life a chance."

Arriving in Palo Alto, we moved into her sister Carole's home and then went to an appointment with Pauline's pulmonary doctor, who wanted to admit her to the hospital to run all the tests necessary to prepare her for possible transplantation. He also wanted to evaluate her seizure condition thoroughly, because it could present a problem during surgery.

Pauline hated being admitted. She always had difficulty getting the extensive sleep she needed whenever she was hospitalized.

I wanted to stay with her, but no private rooms were available so I was not allowed to stay in her room. I tried sleeping in the waiting room, but it was right in the middle of a busy hallway, making sleep nearly impossible. I decided to return to Caroles's for the night.

The next day, Memorial Day, Pauline was already getting exhausted. We arranged for a pass so she could go to Carole's for the day. I put her in bed and she slept several hours. When she awoke I helped her shower and dress, and then I had her sit in a chair. While she visited with her parents, I took another roll of 24 portrait-type photographs.

We all went out to eat before I took Pauline back to the hospital.

Returning to Carole's for the night, I wrote in my journal about how difficult it was spending the night away from Pauline, and then pondered:

> How strange life is! How ambiguous! How uncertain! How fearsome! To work so hard at making our love grow. To be to and for each other what we believe God wants us to be. And then to face the fact that we may be separated. No, not "separated." That's too mild. That we may be "torn apart." The image I

have of our life together being severed is an image of both of us reaching out to each other, grasping for each other, yet forced apart, torn apart, by some power, some force, greater than ourselves.

I can't believe that force is God. God couldn't break our lives apart. The God we love so dearly couldn't do this to us.

And yet God could allow it. Oh theology, how hollow you are now! Oh, theological distinctions, how empty you are now! The distinctions of the mind mean so little when the heart so strongly needs one thing. I need Pauline. I need her presence. I need her to be in this room with me.

God, we have loved as we believe you have wanted us to love. I will not apologize for never wanting to be separated, torn apart, from Pauline. Lord, our love is eternal. You have made it that, with your blessing. For that we praise you, and we ask you to keep us together.

The following day was filled with tests. I had decided to leave in the afternoon and fly from San Francisco to Ontario, California, to pick up our car. I flew out, arrived in Ontario and friends met me there with the car. I then headed back north to Palo Alto.

I found a motel room in the northern Los Angeles area and called the desk on Pauline's hospital floor to tell the nurses where I was for the night.

Early the next morning I was awakened by a phone call. It was Pauline. In the middle of the night she had had a seizure, and been moved to Intermediate Intensive Care. She had been up all night undergoing tests. Pauline was exhausted. She knew if she didn't get some sleep she might have another seizure.

Part of the problem was that Pauline had not been

given her Isuprel throughout the night in the same manner I gave it to her. I had developed a preventive schedule in which I would wake her at certain intervals to slip an Isuprel into her mouth. This had worked quite well to stop any nightly seizures.

I felt angry. I was so afraid this would happen. I told Pauline to rest, not to allow them to test her until she had slept and to let me talk to the nurse in charge. I explained to the nurse what Pauline needed, and I told her to keep all visitors away. Then I jumped in the car and headed straight to Stanford.

This was not the first time, nor would it be the last, that I would have conflict with medical personnel. Stanford University has one of the finest medical centers in the world. Pauline had some of the finest doctors and nurses. But I knew Pauline in a way no stranger could. I could almost tell exactly how she was feeling just by looking into her eyes. All those days together, and all those nights helping her fight off seizures, had taught me what she could tolerate and what she could not. I knew how much sleep she needed, how much stress and physical exertion she could tolerate, how much company she could handle and how important Isuprel was to her breathing.

I knew Pauline from the inside out. This is why I wanted to be with her as much as possible whenever she was in the hospital. Medical personnel know the patient from the outside in. They are working with measurements and statistics, and their experience with the overall progression of a particular disease. However, patients are unique, which makes it difficult for a doctor or nurse to judge precisely their condition.

The reason I had conflict with medical personnel at Dakota Hospital before, and at Stanford now, was because I knew Pauline in a way they never could. There were times when I was wrong about certain things. But there were also many times when I was right. And, with Pauline's health at stake, I was not about to sit by passively and quietly.

Furthermore, a disease like Pauline's was just plain frustrating to everyone involved. There was so little that could be done. We all knew that. Frustration, stress and tiredness often led to short tempers. However, we all knew that we were in this together, hoping and working for the best for Pauline.

Over the next four days more tests continued. Pauline was getting exhausted, but at least I was allowed to sleep in a reclining chair beside her so I could let the nurses know when she needed more Isuprel. I kept begging to bring her home and then back in for outpatient tests. Finally, on Monday, a week after she had been admitted to the hospital for final testing, I was allowed to take her home to Carole's.

I put her in bed and she immediately fell into a peaceful sleep. It was such a joy to be able to hold Pauline as she slept. How good it was again to have her in this room, in this bed, her presence—even while sleeping—adding such life, joy and security to this room.

Soon tears began to well up in my eyes. For Pauline's body, as I held her, felt so weak, so defenseless against the horrible disease she was fighting. Faced with the possibility that one day she could die and never return to this room again, never crawl into bed with me again, never sleep in my arms again, I was filled with such an inexpressible feeling of sorrow.

Over the next few days Pauline began to regain some of her strength and to feel better. We had our beeper, and all systems were "go" for the transplant once a suitable heart-lung became available.

And then Carole informed me that if we were going to continue to live in her house I needed to start doing some chores. She sent me out to do yard work. I spent the afternoon working, my anger growing that I could not be by Pauline's side for whatever she might need.

I decided to rent a two-bedroom apartment, which we would share with Pauline's parents. Once settled, the four of us had many wonderful days together. We took turns cooking things Pauline liked to eat, watched television, played cards and occasionally went out to eat when Pauline was feeling especially strong.

There continued to be occasional tests at the hospital,

including a stress test so they could compare her cardiovascular capacity before surgery to after surgery. I fought against doing this test because I knew she would have a seizure, but the doctors insisted. Sure enough, she had a seizure while trying to walk on the treadmill, collapsed to the floor and the doctors had to perform CPR.

It was now June 18, and no more tests were needed. We could go home to our apartment and wait for the transplant.

A week later Pauline's sister, Gail, arrived from Florida to spend a week with us. They had not seen each other in a year, and they had many wonderful conversations.

Although I enjoyed seeing Pauline have so many meaningful visits with her family, I missed the conversations just the two of us would have in the evenings all those years. And, as the days went by, I had wanted to talk about spirituality, and get a clearer sense of how she was now feeling about that aspect of her journey. However, most nights she was too tired from visiting to have any energy left for such conversations.

Right after Gail left and her parents had gone to bed, we were finally alone. I suggested we take time to talk, but I could also see she was quite tired. Nevertheless, I suggested we needed to talk as I sat on the edge of our bed. Pauline closed her eyes and said, "Please, I need to sleep. I have chest pains."

I felt sick and angry with myself. "Honey, I'm sorry, I'm so sorry," I said. I stroked her hair. "Go to sleep. This isn't important now."

Pauline went right to sleep, and I noticed that she had been reading her book by Meister Eckhart. I picked it up and began to page through it, looking at what Pauline had underlined. I came upon this passage, which Pauline had noted in particular:

> In this life there are two kinds of certainty about
> eternal life. The first is based on the belief that
> God himself tells man about it, or that he sends

word through an angel, or reveals it in some special illumination. These rarely happen, and to few people.

The second kind is incomparably better and more useful and common among people who love wholeheartedly. It is based on the love for God and the intimacy with him which binds man to him, by which he has full confidence in God and is so completely certain of him that he loves God, without making any difference, in all creatures. And even though creatures denied God and forswore him, and even though God denied himself, still he could not mistrust, because love cannot mistrust. Love is confidence itself in the good and therefore there is no need to speak of the Lover and the beloved; for once a man discovers that God is his friend, he knows what is good for him and all that belongs to his happiness. Of this you may be sure, that however dear you are to God, he is immeasurably dearer to you and he trusts you that much more; for he himself is the confidence by which one is sure of him, as sure as all who love him are.

When I finished reading this passage, tears came to my eyes. "Oh preacher man," I thought, "when will you ever learn? You feel you have to talk about what Pauline already knows and feels. You may have a need to talk with her, but she doesn't have that need. Pauline knows God as her friend in whom she can trust. What else is needful?" Once again I witnessed the depth of her faith, the purity of her trust.

The next morning I apologized for creating extra stress for her, and I shared with her what I had read in her book. She simply smiled and said, "That's okay."

June turned to July and Pauline began to regain some strength. On July 4 we went for a drive to check out some golf courses in the area. One of our fantasies was about being able to play golf together again. We found a course that was particularly scenic and reflected on how fun it would be to play it together.

As we drove back to our apartment, fear gripped me once again. Over the years we had driven thousands of miles together in our car, but now a new thought occurred to me. "Honey, I'm so afraid one day I may be driving this car and your seat will be empty." Pauline looked at me sadly and said nothing for a time. Then she reassured me that she thought she would make it through the surgery.

Pauline rested the next two days, and then on July 7 we went to Stanford to tour the transplant area and check in with one of her doctors. He listened to her heart and said there was still good reserve in it. On the way home we toured the area, looking at some of the shops and restaurants we hoped to visit in the near future.

That night, after dinner, Pauline had another seizure. It was becoming clear to me that she was having more and more difficulty recovering from these seizures. The next day, after lunch, she had another seizure. I listened to her pulse. It climbed to 100 and stayed there for an hour and a half. Finally I called her doctors. I was told not to worry unless her pulse went to 120 and would not come down. It stayed at 100 for quite a while longer, but eventually it came down.

That night Pauline had very little appetite. At bedtime she again had difficulty catching her wind. There was so little I could do to help her anymore! Finally, as I held her, stroking her hair, I recited a passage from Isaiah that often had given us strength and hope: "They who wait for the Lord shall renew their strength, they shall mount up with wings like eagles, they shall run and not be weary, they shall walk and not faint." [40:31; RSV]

The tears began to stream down Pauline's cheeks. As she cried, the shortness of breath only got worse. Resolutely she choked back the tears. I felt such rage at this disease that now had taken away both her laughter and her tears!

The next day Pauline stayed in the bed the whole day. Again that night, when she lay down to sleep, she hyperventilated and had great difficulty catching her breath. It wasn't until 1:00 a.m. that she finally was able to fall asleep.

I lay down beside her and a strange feeling came over me in the darkness. I was so aware of her breathing, so aware of her presence. I felt this deep joy, this deep sense of gratitude just having her beside me. The feeling was overwhelming, so much so that I got up and turned on the television, the volume very low, casting just enough light into the room for me to look at her. For an hour I just looked at her, stroked her hair and reflected on her beauty and how much I loved her until I finally fell asleep.

When I awoke the next morning, the feeling again came over me again. Although I was exhausted, and needed to sleep, the beauty of her presence overwhelmed me. For three hours I lay there holding Pauline, playing with her hair, looking at her face, until she finally awoke.

Soon after her pulse shot up and she could not catch her wind. I listened to her heart. Her pulse shot up to 130 and stayed there for a half hour. Then it dropped to 120, but would go no lower. Finally I decided to call an ambulance.

When the paramedics arrived, Pauline asked me not to let them take her to the hospital. "Honey," I said, "you have to go. I just don't know what to do for you anymore." Finally she agreed. We both knew she had no choice.

That night Pauline insisted I go home to get some sleep, and I agreed. When I returned the next morning, she was already up in bed and was alert, smiling at me broadly. She had had another seizure that night, and she had another one that morning. However, she recovered quite well and she did fairly well the rest of the day. Her body was not infected, and that meant, if only donor organs could be found, that she could still have the surgery.

That evening I held Pauline's hand as she tried to relax and go to sleep. As I sat on the chair beside her bed, she kept her head, now greatly elevated to help her breathing, turned toward me as she tried to sleep. I could see she was uncomfortable. Her back was sore from lying on it so much, and her neck seemed sore (she kept moving it in a circle).

Finally I suggested she turn her head and face the other way. Tears began to stream down her face and she quietly said, "But what if I never see you again?"

Tears came to my eyes. "I know, honey, " I said, "but we're going to make it. Just rest. You'll have the transplant."

We talked awhile longer and then Pauline was finally ready to sleep. She looked up at me and said, "Honey, I love you with all my heart and soul and mind. I love you with every inch of my body. I love you now and forever." Then she went to sleep.

That night I slept in a lounge and found her the next morning sitting up and looking quite comfortable. That morning I had finished reading the latest of Pauline's journal entries. I told her how moved I was by them, and then I asked her, "Pauline, if you die, do I have permission to use them in the best way I see fit?" She smiled, and said, "Sure."

About noon I noticed that Pauline seemed rather sullen. I looked at her pulse rate. It was quite low. I asked her if she had any new symptoms. No, she said. Did she want to see a doctor? No. But I could tell something was bothering her. I asked her if something was wrong. No, she replied. Still I could see she was troubled. "Honey, " I said after awhile, "what's wrong?"

She looked straight at me, and again the tears began to roll down her cheeks. "I'm scared. I'm so tired of trying to be strong, but I don't want you to worry."

I began to cry, and I told her how worried I was too. We held each other and quietly sobbed. After awhile Pauline lay back peacefully on her pillow, and she said she felt better. Then I told her how moved I was to be loved by her "now and forever" and how deeply meaningful it was when I read in her journal that she wanted me to know how much she loved me with her "dying heart." Then I said to her, "My heart is dying at the thought of your death."

That afternoon Dr. Jamieson came in to see how Pauline was doing. She tried to smile and talk, but her wind kept getting worse, and she went into another seizure. By now Pauline was receiving her Isuprel intravenously, and Dr.

Jamieson decided to move her into the transplant area. Hoping against hope, I followed Pauline as they rolled her down corridor after corridor. She kept trying to smile at me, but it was difficult for her to do so as she gasped for air.

When she arrived at the Intensive Care wing of the transplant area, the doctors and nurses had difficulty attaching all the monitor leads because Pauline's chest was covered with perspiration. Her breathing kept getting worse. As I had so many times in the past, I tried to cradle her head and hold it up to help her breathe. It did not seem to help. She winced in pain with such a look of agony in her eyes. I knew what was going to happen. I could see it coming on. I told the doctors she was going to have a seizure. They told me not to alarm her but I knew if she had the seizure, her heart would stop.

Suddenly, Pauline's eyes rolled back, her body wrenched into another seizure and her heart stopped! The cardiac resuscitation team rushed in, and I was pushed from the room. I stood in the hallway feeling delirious. Was this a dream? This was exactly the way Pauline did not want to die! After her long and brave fight, would she die in exactly the way she did not want to die?

In the reflection in the window I could see a nurse up on Pauline's bed, her hands pushing rhythmically on Pauline's chest. I remembered Pauline telling me about a book she read on near-death experiences. A person reported that he had come back into his body because someone had called him back and he realized how much that person wanted him back, even though he was drawn to a light. I began praying and calling: "Pauline, if you are there, if you hear me, if you can come back, please come back. Don't give up yet. I need you. Please come back."

Finally, a nurse came out. "She came back. She's alive again."

Dr. Jamieson had been called when Pauline's heart had stopped. He asked me if I wanted to come with him to have some coffee. I asked when I could see Pauline. He told me soon, but not yet. "Stu," I said, "are there any organs available at all? We have to try something. Pauline wants the transplant.

She desperately wants to give her life one more chance."
"No," he said, "there's nothing. Nothing is available."

When I was able to see Pauline, I was shocked by what I saw. She was breathing uncontrollably. It was as if she had just finished a marathon. Her chest was literally heaving! She could not get words out between the gasps for air. I tried to relax her. I held her and stroked her hair and talked to her, telling her how beautiful she was and how much I loved her.

Pauline kept trying to speak. Then I remembered what I had done in the hallway. I felt a little embarrassed as I asked her, "Pauline, did you have an out-of-body experience?" She shook her head no. Well, I thought, so much for that.

I asked her if she wanted Holy Communion, and she nodded yes. I began to prepare the elements, but the doctors asked me to leave so they could put another catheter in her neck. As I waited I could see another seizure overtaking her. Again the cardiac team rushed in and I was rushed out.

I did the only thing I could think to do. Standing outside the door I prayed and called to her. The fight this time did not take as long, as the doctors decided to put her on a respirator. Dr. Jamieson had told me they didn't want to do this unless absolutely necessary, because once Pauline was on the respirator the transplant would have to take place within two days. After that period of time her body would probably become infected.

When I saw Pauline, she looked so uncomfortable. A long tube was going down her mouth and into her trachea, periodically forcing air into her worn-out lungs. Pauline tried to talk, but it was impossible with the respirator. I was determined that we share Holy Communion together right away.

I began to weep, choking out the Words of Institution the best I could. Then I began the Lord's Prayer. I could see Pauline's lips trying to move as she said this holy prayer with me. Then I placed a piece of bread in her mouth beside the respirator tube: "The body of Christ, broken for you." I poured wine into her mouth: "The blood of Christ, shed for you." Then the blessing: "The body of our Lord Jesus Christ and his precious blood strengthen you now and unto life eternal."

I was startled to feel something on my neck. I turned to find that Pauline had raised her weak arm and placed it around my neck. I looked at her and said, "Pauline, give me Communion." I placed a piece of bread in her hand, and slowly she brought it to my mouth. Then I took the small cup and put it in her hand, and she brought it to my lips.

Pauline became extremely animated. She pointed up in the air, and tried to express herself by spelling out words with her index finger. I couldn't understand what she was trying to communicate. Again and again she tried, but I couldn't understand. I felt so frustrated! Finally Dr. Jamieson came over. Pauline pointed to her heart. "Are you experiencing bad chest pains?" he asked. She nodded no. He thought for a moment. "Pauline, are you wondering whether we can still give you the transplant if you hang in there?" She smiled. "Yes," he said. We all stood amazed at her will to live.

Pauline kept trying to communicate to me. Finally I said, "Pauline, do you want me to crawl into bed with you?" She smiled and nodded yes. I don't know if that is what she was trying to tell me, or if that just sounded good to her once I suggested it. In any case, I crawled into bed and held her. One of the nurses said, "What are you doing!" I did not reply, and she said no more.

Eventually an X-ray technician came in and the nurse told me I would have to leave. I tried to get out of bed, but Pauline would not let go of my hand. Finally she consented, and let go of my hand. Then she pointed to herself, "I", then her heart, "love," and then to me, "you."

I went in the waiting room with her parents and began to weep. "This is it, " I cried. "Pauline is going to die. She's not going to make it."

After Pauline's parents left, I went back into Pauline's room. She was sleeping. Finally the morphine had relaxed her into sleep. I asked the nurse what time she thought Pauline would wake up. She said at about 7:00 am.

I sat alone in the lounge all night, in fits of sleep, clutching her journal. I woke up with a start! I looked at my watch and it was 5:30 am. The image of Pauline pointing up into the air came into my mind. What was she trying to tell me? If she died, would I always wonder what she was trying to communicate to me? Then it dawned on me. Was she trying to tell me she had had an out-of-body experience? I hadn't asked her about that after the second cardiac arrest. I raced to her room. I had to ask her. When I arrived, Pauline was soundly asleep. The doctor told me the situation was very bleak. They had tried everything they could think of, but nothing was working. It was nearly hopeless. Her fever was high. She hadn't passed urine for six hours. Her kidneys had apparently stopped working, and her body had become infected.

My stomach knotted! Infection! That meant no transplant!

Then the nurse told me Pauline had been awake just a few minutes before. She had wanted to know where I was, and the nurse had told her I was sleeping in the lounge. Then they had given her more medicine to help her go back to sleep.

Oh no, I thought, Pauline was awake and I wasn't there! What if she died now? The last time she was awake on this earth she would have been alone.

I needed desperately to talk with her again. I needed to be with her the last time she was awake in this life. I had to know if I finally understood what she was trying to communicate to me.

I stood by Pauline's bed, holding her hand, talking softly to her. Looking at the heart monitor, I could see how desperately ill she was. Her heartbeat was terribly arrhythmic, and her pulse was unsteady. It would go very slow, then speed up, and then slow down again.

I prayed and prayed and prayed. "Please God, don't let this be the end. Heal her. Bring life to her broken body."

As she slept, Pauline went into cardiac arrest for the third time. Again, they brought her back, but she was still unconscious. The attending physician told me the situation was entirely hopeless and he didn't feel they should try to revive Pauline anymore. He asked my permission to let her die the next time she had an arrest.

My head swam. Let her die? How could I do that? I told him I couldn't make that decision. I stood there silently for a long time. He insisted it was really unfair to Pauline to continue to allow her to suffer in this way.

I tried to find Dr. Jamieson to ask his opinion but he was in surgery. I called Pauline's parents and asked them to come to the hospital immediately, briefly explaining to them what the situation was.

I went back into Pauline's room and told the doctor that I wanted to ask Pauline what she wanted when she woke up. The doctor told me that he did not think Pauline would regain consciousness.

Those words hit me like a bolt. I would not be able to talk to Pauline again! But I had to! I had to ask her what she wanted. I had to apologize for not being there when she had last been awake. I had to ask her if I finally understood what she had been trying to communicate to me.

I stood at her bed, praying, holding her, stroking her hair, talking to her. I asked her to wake up, to please wake up and talk to me.

Finally her eyelids began to move. Then her eyes slowly opened. I could see she was fighting through the morphine for pure vision. Eventually her eyes focused on me, and she smiled. "Hi honey," I said.

Then I told her to blink once for yes, and twice for no. I asked her if she understood, and she blinked yes.

"Pauline, were you trying to tell me last night that you had an out-of-body experience?" She blinked yes.

"How many did you have? One?" She blinked no. "Two?" She blinked yes. She had had two out-of-body experiences, after the second and third cardiac arrests.

I began to ask her questions about the experiences from what little I knew about such events. Whatever I described, she blinked no.

Finally, I said to her, "Pauline, was the experience positive?" She blinked yes, and then wrinkled her nose (an expression I had seen many times, which meant "sort of"). I tried again. "Was it positive?" Again her answer was ambiguous. I stood there contemplating her response.

Again I tried. "Was it positive?" She answered yes, with a frown. "Did you want to stay?" She answered no. Then it hit me, and I said, "It was positive, but you didn't want to stay because you wanted to come back and be with me?" She blinked yes, and smiled broadly.

I smiled, too, and thanked her for coming back to me. I told her how much I had wanted to talk with her again.

Then I said, "Pauline, do you know that you have had three cardiac arrests?" She blinked yes. I told her how proud I was of her for fighting so courageously.

Then I had to utter what are the most difficult words I have ever spoken. "Honey, as long as you're alive there is hope, but you're not doing very well. Your body is infected. They can no longer do the transplant."

Into her eyes came the deepest look of sadness I have ever seen. I know her body must have been telling her it was all over, but it was as if she could not accept that fact until she heard those words from me.

We stared at each other in pain. The worst that we had envisioned had now happened, and there was nothing we could do about it. I longed to know what Pauline wanted to say. If only she could talk!

Then I told her that the doctors expected her to have another cardiac arrest soon, and they had asked me if they should try to revive her. "Honey," I said, "It goes against everything in my whole being to consider allowing them not to revive you. Pauline, what do you want? If you have another arrest, do you want them to try to revive you?"

She blinked yes, and smiled. I looked at the nurse beside us, and asked her if she had seen that. The nurse smiled and nodded yes.

Then I said to Pauline: "So, you like coming back and talking to me?" She smiled and blinked yes. I told her that they would try to revive her and that I would be there as long as she wanted to fight. Then I said, "Pauline, thank you for coming back again and again. Thank you for being so strong for us. I'll be here as long as you want to fight. But from now on you do what you want to do." She nodded that she understood.

We talked awhile longer, but soon I could see she was beginning to drift off. As her eyes closed, I said the words we had parted with so many times before: "I love you with all my heart. Always have. Always will!"

Her heart stopped for the fourth time. I stepped back from the bed as the staff asked me what they should do. "Try to revive her," I said. "That is what she wanted. But this time I don't think she's coming back."

In a matter of moments Pauline lay dead before me. She was 31. I held her and kissed her and stroked her hair and thanked her for the gracious, undying love she had given me.

I knew she could truly say, with the Apostle Paul, "I have fought the good fight, I have finished the race, I have kept the faith." [II Timothy 4:7; RSV]

Pauline's last journal entry was on May 22:

> I'm alive now. Please help me make the most of it. I do not want to spend what might be my last days bitter, depressed, or sullen. I want to leave Bear with good remembrances of me.

> I do not seem to laugh anymore. Is it because I get out of wind, or is the great expert on death and dying having trouble coping? Whatever the reason, I want to leave with a smile on my face.

> My theology, please don't desert me now. It would be much easier to be a radical right-winger—to say this is all God's will. But I believe that God doesn't cause suffering and that many times s/he does not interfere. Thus, if I am dying, let God's tears be enough. It is enough.

God, please make my heart less heavy. Is the burden death, or is it lethargy from illness?

God, I want to be like Eckhart and say, "Your will be done." But I don't want to die. I just want to talk to you about my tears.

Part III

The Long Journey Home

Chapter 9   Blue Flowers, Blue Casket

Storybook endings
Never appear
They're just someone's way of
Leading us here.
--Dan Fogelberg, "The Innocent Age"

"Brian, Brian, I am so sorry. So very sorry!"

Walking out of the hospital I turned to see Mary Burge, the social worker on the transplant team, running after me. I was rolling a wheelchair down the hallway with Pauline's "effects," as we say. What a term for the belongings left behind by a loved one who has died! Tied to the wheelchair were two helium filled balloons given to Pauline by a woman in the pulmonary lab who had a special bond with her.

Tears were streaming down Mary's face. She told me how terribly sorry she was. We talked for a while. I shared some of Pauline's journal with her, and then walked to my car. As I started to pull out of the parking lot, I turned and smashed one of the balloons. It popped, the rubber falling to the floor. I looked at it. Broken rubber. A dead balloon. Dead like Pauline. Dead like all my dreams.

I drove to our apartment. Pauline's parents greeted me with hugs and tears. We sat down, and in a state of shock, talked about the past few hours.

Then I went to our bedroom. I stood in the doorway and looked around. I was flooded with memories of being there with Pauline. Each of her belongings made my heart ache.

That night I wrote in my journal:

July 13, 1982

It was hard for me to leave Pauline's body. It was hard to look at her for the last time, and leave. I kept wanting to look one more time. Finally I made up my mind that I just had to go. I looked at her, and left.

I'm surprised I haven't cried more today. I've been busy with practical matters, such as funeral arrangements and plans to leave Palo Alto. I guess I'm numb, or too exhausted to really feel.

I'm partly buoyed by the fact that I was able to talk with, cry with and hold and kiss my dear Pauline throughout her four cardiac arrests. What we shared will give me deep meaning eternally. Perhaps the clear memory of her presence so recently with me is uplifting me.

But when I fall, which will be soon, I'm going to come crashing down. Pauline, I love you with all my heart, always have, always will. Oh, how my heart aches!

July 14, 1982

The dam did burst. When I finally went to bed, I convulsed in sorrow. The reality that you weren't there and wouldn't ever be again, honey, shattered me. I cried uncontrollably. After awhile I took a short walk, and then fell exhausted into a restless sleep.

Stu Jamieson called this afternoon. We talked a good half-hour. He was really moved by Pauline. "Deeply moved" is the way he put it. She is the epitome of why they have such a transplant program. He said that if in his whole career he saved one person like Pauline, he would feel it was worth his effort as a doctor.

He was truly amazed by her will to live. He told me the normal person would have probably died a month before. He said it is really frustrating trying to find donors, and that a lot of the problem is public awareness. He would like me to write about Pauline in hopes that something could be printed that would let people know how desperate the situation is, and what it means in human terms when donors are not available. He also asked for a picture of Pauline.

The next day I rented a U-Haul trailer and packed up our belongings. Brother Alan flew into Oakland from Bismarck. I picked him up that evening and we prepared for the long drive back to Hemet the next morning.

Pauline had said her love for me was undying. I believed it and I felt it. Somehow I was still able to function because she loved me and because I had to go home to meet her body. I wanted to plan a funeral just right for her that both proclaimed my grief and yet witnessed to her courage, faith and undying love for God's world.

On the way back to Hemet we stopped at the American Lutheran Church synod office in Thousand Oaks to visit with Rev. Howie Wennes, Assistant to the Bishop, whom I had asked to preach at Pauline's funeral. I left him copies of several of Pauline's journal entries.

As we drove into the driveway of our home, I realized it would be my first time in the house without her. How painful the "first times" are. I walked through each room in our home, feeling overcome with loneliness, emptiness, sadness, fear. No Pauline. Just her things. Just our things.

Soon people starting arriving, which is the most meaningful thing when you are in the throes of grief. I can't remember any specific things said to me when I was grieving, but I do remember the people who showed up. The presence of people who love us and care about us is the greatest comfort we can receive in times of loss.

First Pauline's parents arrived from Palo Alto, along with

Pauline's sisters. Then came friends from seminary. These friends were willing to lament with me, which is what I desperately needed at that point. I felt, as I wrote in my journal, that "too many people are just too accepting of Pauline's death. Right away they wax into pious phrases and sentimental theology. Pauline is over her suffering. She is with her Lord. She is healed now. I know all that. And I'm happy for Pauline. But I'm not happy for me. I'm not happy for the world. I'm not happy for the part of Pauline that wanted so badly to live longer in this world, and fought so courageously for that life."

I felt such frustration, depression and anger at the unfairness of it all. I didn't blame God for Pauline's death--she didn't believe God willed it, and neither did I. But there was such a fundamental injustice in Pauline's death, for her, for me, for the world. We didn't want to be separated, and we shouldn't be.

I hoped others would join me in lamenting her. "Please," I wrote, "don't accept the tragedy of Pauline's death so quickly, so easily. Cry with me. Scream with me. Walk with me through this grief that feels so unbearable." We had been torn apart, and I wanted to scream because of the agony of that separation.

When we are in the throes of grief, it feels unbearable. We want the pain to be over, but not at the cost of diminishing the importance, the tragedy, of our loss. When I was a young boy my Cub Scoutmaster died at a young age. I still remember that funeral vividly.

During it his wife began to wail. My first feeling was embarrassment. Adults are not supposed to do that in public. Now, all these years later, I finally understood the clash of personal pain and our cultural norms when it comes to what is considered appropriate displays of emotion in public.

I fell into another restless sleep and awoke the morning of the funeral, July 19, 1982 feeling a sense of nervousness. I wanted everything to be just right. We are powerless to stop the deaths of those we love, so we channel all that frustrated energy into trying to make the funeral just right.

People kept stopping by and I greeted them as best I could. The funeral was at 2:00 pm, and time seemed to pass so slowly. I decided I didn't want to wait for everyone else to get ready, so at 1:00 pm I walked the six blocks to church. As I did, I kept uttering to myself: "I'm coming to get you, Pauline. I'm coming for you."

I found Pauline, in her blue casket open for viewing in the fellowship hall. I wanted to be alone with her, but already there were people everywhere. Finally, right before the service, Pauline's family and I had a chance to be alone with Pauline before the casket was closed. As difficult as it was, I knew I had to look at her one last time, and then let the lid be shut forever. It is good that we do that right before the service—with hundreds of people waiting—or else we might never let the casket be closed.

Into the sanctuary we marched, following the casket, as we joined the congregation in singing the entrance hymn:

> The King of love my shepherd is,
>   Whose goodness faileth never;
> I nothing lack if I am his
>   And he is mine forever.
>
> In death's dark vale I fear no ill,
>   With thee, dear Lord, beside me,
> Thy rod and staff my comfort still;
>   Thy cross before to guide me.
>
> And so through all the length of days,
>   Thy goodness faileth never.
> Good Shepherd, may I sing thy praise
>   Within thy house forever.

What many people do not understand about the liturgy and hymns of the church is that they often do not describe where we are in the present, but rather try to point us to where we hope to be in the future. It is like we are gently prodding ourselves to find a sign of hope in our despair, a ray of sunshine in our darkness.

Pastor Wennes preached, his sermon titled "Triumph of Grace," on the following two passages:

> He gives power to the faint, and strengthens the powerless. Even youths will faint and be weary, and the young will fall exhausted; but those who wait for the Lord shall renew their strength, they shall mount up with wings like eagles, they shall run and not be weary, they shall walk and not faint. [Isaiah 40:29-31; NRSV]

> I have fought the good fight, I have finished the race, I have kept the faith. From now on there is reserved for me the crown of righteousness, which the Lord, the righteous judge, will give me on that day. [II Timothy 4:7-8b; NRSV]

The words he preached have stuck with me all these years:

> A funeral is also a memorial service: a time to remember and honor a sister in Christ. Pauline Peterson Erickson, wife, daughter, sister, friend, believer, child of God, member of the family of faith, an Easter person. Pauline. We remember her as a beautiful woman with a courageous and trusting faith and a passion for life. We remember her as a loving wife who shared her highest hopes and deepest fears with Brian and who pledged the most intimate and tender love "until death us do part." We remember her a precious and deeply loved daughter who knew the devotion of a parents' love and was shaped and nurtured by that love. Pauline, a sister and friend who knew how to love and to express concern and who was not too proud to also receive it in return. Her commitment to being a social worker was also a significant sign

of her caring and compassion; some of the compassion of Jesus Christ and his love rubbed off on her.

Pastor Wennes then shared a few of Pauline's journal entries, concluding with Pauline's Easter entry about Friday, Saturday and Sunday, and then he said:

Pauline was a remarkable woman, a powerful witness to the love of God in relationship to Jesus Christ. Not a trace in her journal of bitterness or despair. There was pain but love was greater. There was regret that the time was too short but hope was greater. There was frustration over her illness but her faith in God was greater.

Then he turned to me:

I believe you shared and experienced the depth of love with her that some people never know even if they live to be 100. We thank God for her ten years as a wife and her 32 years as a daughter and a woman of God. The depth of love that surrounded her was but a glimmer and a glimpse of how much she was loved by her Heavenly Father and her Lord who went to the cross for her and the Spirit who sustained her as she walked through the valley of the shadow.

Her Heavenly Father, like her earthly parents, watched over her and whispered in her ear: "My baby, my dear." Brian, in the favorite and tender greeting and benediction that you and Pauline shared for ten years we find a great summary of the Gospel, of God's passion for his people. And a beautiful expression of the sentiments and commitments that God also has for Pauline. "I love you with all my heart, always have, always will."

We know that God who loves her so deeply will take care of her now and we entrust her to the hands of the Easter Lord as we now live for a season without her.

Once again we followed Pauline's casket, this time out of the sanctuary as we sang:

Lord, be my consolation;
  Shield me when I must die;
Remind me of thy Passion
  When my last hour draws nigh.
These eyes, new faith receiving,
  From thee shall never move;
For he who dies believing,
  Dies safely in thy love.

Now, for the third time in my life, I climbed into a car to follow the casket of a family member I adored to the cemetery and a double plot I had just purchased. Once again the committal service. Once again the Lord's Prayer. Once again dust sprinkled on the coffin, the words of finality breaking the hushed silence:

In sure and certain hope of the resurrection to eternal life through our Lord Jesus Christ, we commend to almighty God our sister, Pauline Marie Peterson Erickson, and we commit her body to the ground; earth to earth, ashes to ashes, dust to dust. The Lord bless her and keep her. The Lord make his face to shine on her and be gracious to her. The Lord look upon her with favor and give her peace.

As people began to file away from the grave, the funeral director motioned me toward a car to ride back to my house for the reception. But I just couldn't leave. I felt driven to stay. I felt compelled to remain until the burial was complete.

It didn't feel right to leave at this surreal point of our funeral customs, with a pretty casket hovering on a stand over a hole you can't see because it is covered with artificial grass.

In spite of the funeral director's protests, I told him to invite everyone to our home. I was staying. I was going to be present and participate in the final part of the burial. I removed the wreath, and watched them lower her body into the earth. As the casket descended I threw blue flowers from the wreath onto it. Then the funeral director gave me a shovelful of dirt to throw into her grave and I watched a truck back up and dump a load of dirt on top of her casket.

There were no tears. They were replaced by a deep feeling of emptiness, of loss. As her body lay in a cold, blue casket beneath concrete and earth I realized how separated we really were.

I remembered a poster we once purchased: "You and me against the world. Frankly, I think we're going to get creamed." It had happened. The world had come between us. It had brought metal and dirt and concrete between us. I had never felt so lonely, so empty. "It's over," I wrote to her. "It's really over. But I'm not over you. And I never will be."

Chapter 10   Empty Home, Empty World

Living in the shadows
Of the things that might have been
Torn between the blessing and the curse
You may stop the hunger
But you'll never slake the thirst
For the nectar you remember
But you'll never taste again.
--Dan Fogelberg, "The Lion's Share"

By the rivers of Babylon—
   there we sat down and wept
   when we remembered Zion.
On the willows there
   we hung up our harps.
How could we sing the Lord's song
   in foreign land?
  --Psalm 137:d1-2, 4; NRSV

"Brian, you go ahead and take as much time as you need," my ministry partner, Pastor Don, said after I told him I couldn't go back to work yet, and that I needed to go home to the Midwest.

The days between death and the funeral are days of shock. We are suspended between disbelief and reality in a way that partially numbs us to the real pain inside. That is good, I guess, because we surely couldn't handle all the pain at once.

They are also days of amazing energy. Driven to get the funeral just right and uplifted by the outpouring of love and compassion, we make many decisions, receive phone calls and visits, work on all the funeral arrangements and read cards and letters.

How ill-prepared we are for the "day after," when the decisions are over, the people are gone, and our "new life" begins—a new life we abhor and fear.

As friends kept leaving I realized I could not return to work yet. I couldn't force myself back into my "normal way" of life. I needed to return to my roots, to where most of Pauline's and my life had been lived. I wanted to go back to Bismarck, Fargo, St. Paul, not only for the support of family and friends, but to face directly and right away the memories that resided in the places that were special to us.

I knew enough about grieving to know that you can't go over it, under it or around it. Healing only comes by going straight "through" it, as painful as that is.

After talking to Don, I spoke with the leaders of the congregation about heading home for several weeks, and I told them they didn't have to pay me, and they didn't. Every time I share that it results in laughter. I am not sure exactly why. I guess just because we all recognize that, while we may be in the throes of loss and grief, the world just keeps going on.

I still remember when Pauline was near death at Dakota Hospital in Fargo in 1980, I was so stressed I decided to buy a pack of cigarettes. I went across the street to a convenience store, where I had to stand in line. I remember thinking to myself: "Don't these people know what I am going through? How can they make me stand in line and go about their lives, joking and laughing?"

Alan continued to be a real trooper, taking time from his job to heed my request to stay with me, including driving back to North Dakota together. We stopped in Las Vegas, and spent Pauline's 32nd birthday playing 92 holes of golf in 100-degree heat. Nothing is much fun in grief, but I did find that whatever little comfort there was to be had, besides being with friends, was to be found in playing my favorite sport.

Arriving in Bismarck, I visited with Pauline's parents and Joel Gilbertson, my college roommate who was now an attorney there. I then headed to Fargo to visit several friends, and then to the Minnesota lakes to be with the Haukness family.

Returning to West Fargo, Pastor Thor from the church where I had served my first four years in ministry, suggested that we have a memorial service there. I loved that idea, as we had so many friends in the congregation, and because so many of our friends and family had not been able to travel to Hemet for the funeral.

I spent the week visiting friends in Fargo, sharing Pauline's journal with them. There were lots of tears, lots of laughter. Each night I found a little piece of healing for my broken heart. Each retelling of stories, each sharing of memories, each tear shed, brings a touch of healing that chips away at the mountain of grief.

I decided that for the memorial service I would try to read some of Pauline's journal entries myself. Having read them several times to others, I thought that by now I would be able to do it myself in public.

I asked Pastor Elmo, who was now in Fargo, to preach. I don't know how fair it is to ask any preacher to preach at the funerals of three of your family members, but I did it anyway, and he, as always, consented.

The sanctuary was filled with members of Faith, including many of the youth with whom Pauline and I had worked, life-long family friends from Maddock and friends from many other places. Once again I was uplifted by the enormous love and concern of so many caring people.

But of course the grief remained. As I looked at pictures of Pauline, I felt so helpless, so alone. I wanted to reach out and hold her and kiss her, but I no longer could. All I had were pictures and memories. And her journal. That was so much. But it felt so much less than Pauline's actual presence.

I loved her so much that sometimes I wished death would come. I wanted to cross over to her, writing, "But there can be no crossing over without the cross. Pauline bore her cross so well and now I have to bear mine. Oh, Christ, please help me. Help me bear this heavy load. Help me carry this unbearable feeling of loss and grief. Give me hope. Help me find new meaning on this earth until the day I join you eternally and hold my dear Pauline again."

Finally I knew it was time to head back to California, as much as I did not want to. I asked my friend, Howard, to go with me so I wouldn't have to drive alone. On the journey back, I had a nightmare of Pauline dying while I tried to save her. I yelled out for someone to call the paramedics, but no one answered. I awoke in a sweat as the thought went through my mind that Pauline was dying in my arms and I could do nothing. And no one was there to help us.

I lay in bed, agonizing over the feeling of helplessness I felt in that dream. The same feeling of helplessness I felt so often as Pauline's illness got worse, and as she died.

Eventually I went back to sleep and I dreamed about Pauline again. Often since, I have wondered if it really was a dream. In the dream I was sleeping in the actual motel in which I was staying. Pauline was sitting on the next bed looking at me. I awoke from sleep and saw her sitting there, with such a loving smile as she looked at me. I felt such indescribable joy. Pauline had not really died! She was here with me again! I sat up, and a tremendous desire to touch her and hold her came over me. I leaned over to hold her, but as I did, a deep, sad look came into her eyes, as if she was saying, "I want you to hold me, but you cannot." As I reached for her my mind began to race. Is this a dream or isn't it. Is Pauline alive, or isn't she? I reached for her. As I came near her, my eyes opened and she was gone.

It was as if she had come to me from eternity. As if she wanted me to know how deeply she loved me. As if she wanted me to know she understood how much I missed her and that she had not chosen to leave me.

I got out of bed and got dressed in a daze. I was silent all morning. Finally, about an hour out of town, I shared my dream with Howard. We were both silent as the tears streamed down our faces. As painful as the dream was, there was a healing message in it. Pauline was okay. And her love was reaching out to try to heal me, to help me go on with my life.

Confused as I was, I knew I had had an experience like

Mary Magdalene. She goes to the tomb to see the body of Jesus, but he is not there. He appears to her, but she does not recognize him, until he calls her by name, "Mary."

At that point we can well picture Mary wanting to run to Jesus and embrace him. However, he stops her and says, "Don't touch me, for I haven't yet ascended to my Father." [John 20:17; HNV]

Over the years people have asked me if I think this was a dream, or if Pauline "really" appeared to me. I "really" don't know the answer. What I do believe is that, either way, Pauline was letting me know she was okay, but that I had to move on without her. I did not fully understand that then, but as time went on I could see more clearly what a gift of grace and love this encounter was, and how significant it was as a beginning act of healing.

We arrived in Hemet on my birthday, August 30, and celebrated (so to speak) by going to dinner at a new Mexican restaurant that had become a favorite of Pauline and me. Returning home, we listened to the 10th Anniversary tape.

The next day we played golf, of course, and that night I drove Howard to the airport for a red-eye flight back to Wisconsin. Arriving at my home at 2:00 am, exhausted, I fell into a restless sleep on this, my first night at home alone.

The next morning I dragged myself into work. I was so anxious, so uncomfortable, so aware of how different my life was now. In a way it was good to be back at work, to have a routine to keep me going, but at the same time it was so agonizing. The same office. The same desk, piled high with mail from weeks gone by. I wanted it to be like it was before with Pauline at home, excited for me to come home for lunch.

I welcomed lunchtime. I needed to get away from the office. I went home as usual but at the door I panicked. I was so afraid to open it. I knew the house would be empty.

I walked into the living room. Empty. I walked into the bathroom. Empty. I walked into our bedroom. Empty. I walked through the entire house. Empty.

I lay down on the couch and I wept. I couldn't eat. Like our home, my life felt empty. Entirely empty.

Somehow I made it through the afternoon, and for dinner I managed to eat a deli sandwich, returning to church for an evening meeting.

But if I thought I had consumed my daily dose of feeling empty, I was sorely mistaken. I was about to discover that, however difficult the day, night was far worse. Driving up to that dark house alone was the ultimate in emptiness.

As a pastor, evening meetings are common. However, Pauline would always make sure the porch light was on for me when I came home, and that came to symbolize a beacon of her welcoming love. As her health continued to deteriorate, she reached the point where she could no longer make it to the light switch for the porch light, but there would still be a light on in the living room, welcoming me home.

It is hard to adequately describe the pain of the reality, beginning to sink in, that my house would always be dark at night. There would be no welcoming light. There would be no Pauline waiting for me. I could inspect every corner of the house and it would be empty.

As I entered the dark house on that first night back, I knew it was not healthy for me to be alone. Most of our friends were busy taking care of children and getting ready for bed themselves.

Then I thought of Chuck, our new friend who was single. I called his house. "Chuck," I said, "I don't know if you are busy tonight, but I don't want to be alone."

Those few words were some of the most important words I would speak. Chuck not only came over that evening, but we would spend many evenings together that coming year. We would develop a deep friendship that would be one of the most important factors in getting me through the year ahead.

The next few days, through my journal and visiting with Chuck, I struggled to come to terms with what had happened to me. I talked about Dad--how I had deserted him in his illness, the guilt I felt for years afterwards, how that guilt was finally healed in Boston and how I had raced home to celebrate with Pauline.

I related how Pauline had commented more than once that I talked about Dad often, but seldom about Mom, and when I did so, I was much more negative. I was angry that she left Alan and me.

This always bothered Pauline. Many times she told me how close she felt to Ruth, and so many times she tried to make me talk about Mom. But through all those conversations the anger continued.

I shared how one night the previous April Pauline persisted in encouraging me to talk about Mom. For hours I talked. Finally I looked at Pauline, and I smiled, "Honey," I said, "you are right. I have been too hard on Mom. Maybe she simply loved Dad so much that she couldn't help feeling that life was so much less meaningful without him." I marveled that Pauline, even while she was dying, was so concerned about me that she wanted to help me reconcile my feelings with Mother.

One noon that first week back I came home from work at noon with no appetite and lay down on the couch and cried. And then the words flowed out of me in a totally uncontrolled manner. "Mom, I love you. I love you so much. Now I understand. Finally I understand the unbelievable emptiness you must have felt when Dad died. Mom, I'm sorry for being angry at you. I love you so much. I need you so much. Dad, I love you so much. I miss you so much. Pauline, I love you so much. I miss you so terribly. I feel so alone. So empty. The three most important people in my life are dead. They are gone. Why must I live without the three people who loved me so much?'"

Finally the tears subsided. I lay still, totally drained. And then it occurred to me. I had addressed Mom first. I had cried out to her first. Then Dad. Then Pauline. Finally I was beginning to understand the deep emptiness that Mom had experienced when Dad died. She is the one who, like me, had to try to go on living without her beloved.

Even after death Pauline continued to heal me. She not only gave me herself, she gave my parents back to me. She made me face the guilt, the anger. She made the four of us one.

I rejoiced in the healing, that eternal togetherness, but I ached over our separation. It was good to be reconciled. But was it enough? How could I go on in this life without the three people who really understood me, who really loved me, who made my life worth living? How could I live with this terrible void that is in my life?

Fortunately for me, friends invited me to dinner the next couple of nights, which helped get me to Sunday when I returned to worship at Trinity Lutheran for the first time in two months. I was greatly moved by the expressions of warmth and consolation that I received. After dinner with friends that night, I went to Pauline's grave. That grave, which I visited over and over again, became my place of both grief and eventually healing.

When Pauline died, her parents wanted to bury her back in Bismarck. I nixed that idea without much discussion. I knew deep inside me that I had to have Pauline near me. I had to be able to go repeatedly to her grave, not primarily for the ritual of bringing flowers, but so that I could talk with her, share my day with her and try to begin to figure out what spiritually God had in mind for me next.

I soon developed another kind of ritual. I would start at the foot of Pauline's grave, facing her. Slowly I would move in a counter-clockwise circle around her grave, calling this my "circle of love." As I did so I would share my feelings and ask her what I should do about certain things.

I have never heard God's voice, and I never heard Pauline's, but through intense prayer and reflection I would listen for and look for guidance and insight.

That first Sunday night back in Hemet, after visiting Pauline's grave, I struggled in my journal with what it meant to still be alive:

> My life is meaninglessness. It has no purpose. I
> stagger through the days like a robot—going
> through the motions, but with no emotions, no
> inspiration, no commitment, no heart.

Because my heart is gone. When Pauline's heart died, so did mine. My heart is in her grave.

Tonight, as I stood by that grave, I looked at the plot beside Pauline's, the plot that is mine. I wanted to lie down beside her. I wanted to lay beside her, close my eyes and pull the earth over me.

I wanted to be with her. I ache so badly to be with her that I feel I would welcome death now.

God, where are you? Pauline asked that of you once. What did you tell her? What are you telling me? Why am I alive? What am I alive for? Why can't Pauline and I be together? Why do I want to die? Is my love for her deeper than my love for life? Is that wrong? Is it wrong to love someone more than life itself?

I am a broken man, a broken man without meaning, drawn again and again to a grave, to the grave of my beloved. I stand there and weep and stand there and cry out. I stand there and want to die.

God, help me. God, restore my life. Somehow, some way, make me want to live again. Heal this unbelievable brokenness I feel. Give me a reason to live.

The next day was the beginning of the bi-annual American Lutheran Church National Convention, being held, fortunately for me, nearby in San Diego. I knew this would be a good opportunity to see many old friends from around the country. While there, I talked to the editor of "The Lutheran Standard," the official magazine of the American Lutheran Church. I discussed with him writing an article, built around Pauline's journal entries, about her experience facing death. I also talked to John Ylvisaker, who produced a Lutheran radio program that used contemporary music along with interviews to deal with key issues of the day. We discussed the possibility of doing a program about Pauline, focusing on the need for organ donors.

I went back to Hemet to work for a couple of days and write a draft of the article for The Lutheran Standard. I returned to San Diego with the article, and taped an interview with Ylvisaker for the radio program. All in all, my time in San Diego was an important step in my healing process. Visiting with friends, writing the article and doing the radio interview, convinced me I had an important story to tell. The desire to share it gave me some much-needed energy and direction.

When someone dear to us dies, we not only struggle to find meaning in our lives without their earthly presence, but we seem to have an innate need for their suffering and death to somehow make a difference. You see this following suicide, or a school shooting or when someone dies from a disease with no known cure. Families get involved in suicide prevention, gun control legislation, raising money for medical research.

For me, I found meaning in sharing the story of Pauline's faith in the midst of suffering, and promoting the need for organ donation, as Dr. Jamieson had requested of me.

I continued this newfound mission the next Sunday when I preached my first sermon since Pauline's death. I titled my sermon "Is it Enough?"

> Pauline, my dear wife, died on July 13 at the age of 32. How does one preach when the feeling of grief is so much a part of his life? What can someone who feels such loss, such emptiness, say to you?

> I have struggled with these questions, and I have concluded that I must look beyond myself—that I must somehow look beyond my experience, my present feelings and try to discover that which can carry me on—that which can give me hope.

Perhaps together we can find the hope that we all need to carry us through our sorrows, our fears, our frustrations, our feelings, at times, of emptiness and meaninglessness.

Our hope is in God's love and God's grace. This is the Good News we proclaim again and again in the church. I need again and again to appropriate that message and you need that message too.

I then went on to talk about how Pauline understood God's love and grace in her life, sharing many of her journal entries and describing the last days of her life. I concluded my sermon:

The question Pauline faced is the question we all face. Is it enough? God does not guarantee that we will not suffer. God doesn't guarantee that we will always be healed of every illness. God doesn't guarantee that we will never die.

For many this is not enough. Many assert that they will only follow God if God protects them from all the pain and tragedy of life.

But God does promise always to stand beside us. God promises never to forsake us, and to always be present with us in our suffering, giving us courage to face that suffering and courage to face death.

Is it enough? Many answer "No, it is not enough." Pauline answered "Yes, it is enough." This is her witness to us. She expressed that belief many times, including in her last journal entry, which was on May 22, with which I conclude.

I then read her journal entry about Holy Week as a microcosm of life.

That first sermon, as difficult as it was to write and to preach, felt like another step along my new direction in life. However, it did not take long for a roadblock to present itself. The word leaked back to me that there were rumblings about the sermon, and I was told by a staff member that someone had said they had not expected to come to worship and end up at a memorial service.

It is difficult to state how painful such comments are! You are working so hard at getting back on your feet, using your newfound insight for good, and then you realize that not everyone is supportive in the way you had hoped. Not only was it painful, it was confusing.

Like a good, reserved Norwegian, I pulled in my pride and tried to get back down to business. In that process I made some good decisions and some poor ones.

The poor ones were that I never looked to join a support group of others who were grieving, nor did I go to professional counseling. At that point in my life I had not matured beyond the notion that strong men don't need professional, psychological counseling (an idea I was surrounded with growing up). Having gone to several counselors since, I now realize what I was missing, and I am sure I stunted my own recovery by neglecting this opportunity.

Secondly, through working over the years with support groups for those who are grieving, I have seen the tremendous value in surrounding yourself with others who have gone through what you are going through. They offer support, understanding and a safe place in which to keep working through whatever is troubling you.

As for good decisions, they included asking Chuck for help, continuing to accept offers to have dinner with friends who wanted to keep up with how I was doing, playing not only golf but also tennis and softball, going regularly to Pauline's grave, and, most importantly, continuing to journal on a regular basis.

That journaling was often morbid and repetitive, but it was the process that kept me on a track towards healing, and it was the main vehicle through which I received insights as to what would bring me further healing. Journaling is strangely revelatory in that way. Unlike a diary, where you objectively record the events of the day, journaling grows out of our emotional interiority, and often our subconscious, bringing to the light of day revelations and insights that slowly heal us and give us hope.

And so, as I kept visiting Pauline's grave, and journaling, I struggled with how to view and understand the great pain and emptiness I felt:

September 18, 1982

So many people misunderstand what I want, what I need. I want healing. But I do not want to be healed.

When you receive a gash on your face you want to be healed. You want it to be totally covered up, leaving no scar. I do not want the gash in my heart where Pauline was to be totally healed. I just want the gaping wound to begin to close.

I have a hole in my heart for Dad. Once it was a gaping wound. Much healing has now taken place, but there is still a hole in my heart where Dad was. The hole causes me pain, but it also reminds me of how much Dad loved me, and how much I love him.

I have a hole in my heart for Mom. It also was once a gaping wound. That wound still bleeds at times, but not as badly as it once did. The pain of that bleeding will never go away. I don't want it to. It reminds me of how much she loved me, and how much I love her.

I don't want to forget Pauline. I don't want to have amnesia. But I don't want to always feel such grief, such loss, such emptiness and such indescribable pain.

I need healing. Now the wound bleeds and bleeds. It leaves me weak, sapping my strength, sapping my energy, sapping my will to live and to love.

I do not want the wound to be healed. I just want to be able to function. I just want to find meaning, fulfillment.

I have been loved. I have been graciously accepted and cared for. I am loved. The holes in my heart constantly remind me of that. God, never close those holes. Never let me forget. I can live with the pain. But I cannot live with the meaninglessness and emptiness that would result if I ever forget, if those holes are ever completely healed.

But please ease the pain. Ease the bleeding. Give me strength. Give me courage. Renew me. Help me to care again. Help me to love, even as I have been loved.

As another step in trying to directly face the pain, near the end of September I played through our 10th Anniversary tape one more time, and then added one, last song:

> Some say love, it is a river,
> That drowns the tender reed.
> Some say love, it is a razor,
> That leaves the soul to bleed.
> Some say love, it is a hunger,
> An endless, aching need.
> I say love, it is a flower,
> And you, its only seed.
>
> It's the heart afraid of breaking,
> That never learns to dance.
> It's the dream, afraid of waking,
> That never takes the chance.

It's the one who won't be taken,
Who cannot seem to give,
And the soul afraid of dying,
That never learns to live.

When the night has been too lonely,
And the road has been too long.
And you think that love is only,
For the lucky and the strong.
Just remember in the winter,
Far beneath the bitter snows,
Lies the seed that with the sun's love,
In the spring, becomes the rose. [Amanda
McBroom and Lincoln Mayorga]

On the last day of September I went to Pauline's grave again and then returned home to journal about the rage I felt inside of me, asking: "Why do I feel such rage? I suppose the answer is simple: because I have lost so much. But where do I direct this rage?"

I explored the possibility of being angry at God, but recognized that Pauline didn't feel that way, nor did I now.

I then reflected on our family and friends. Whenever loss occurs, we are usually surprised by how our friends and family respond: some we thought would be there for us cannot find a way to be present in the way we need. And others will step up in ways we never thought possible. And so I wondered if I should place my rage "on the friends who could not stand by Pauline as she died, who cannot stand by me now as I grieve." Reflecting further on that possibility, I wrote:

But do I really want to do that? Something feels wrong about that. What is it that feels wrong? I'm not sure, but I do have some clues.

Pauline's life was a life of love, of mercy, of gracious acceptance—of me, of others. Her life is a story about love, a story about healing, the powerful healing of the spirit and of relationships that only God can bring.

I want to tell her story. How do I tell it and still express my rage? Will it do any good to lambast the friends who deserted us? No, it won't. No, it can't. It just doesn't fit. I feel that Pauline's story is a story about forgiveness, reconciliation, hope against hope and love. It doesn't fit to be angry with our friends who deserted us. It doesn't fit to be angry with those who have, in my mind, let me down.

Wasn't it I who deserted my Father as he died? Was it because I didn't love him? No, it was because I didn't know what to say. It was because I loved him so much I couldn't bear to see him suffer and die.

Could it be that our friends are no different? That they couldn't stand by Pauline because they loved her so much?

There is no consolation in bitterness. Pauline taught me that. Somehow I must let the rage go. And I want to let it go without unfairly placing it on others who don't deserve it, who don't need it.

God, please heal the loss, please heal the brokenness. Take away the rage, the anger. God, let me say with Pauline, "Let your tears be enough."

Chapter 11   A Heart in a Tomb

Fury rages through your restless day
Shades of time that's gone before
Empty cages where the prisoner plays
'Til the door swings closed behind for evermore . . .
Evermore . . .
Evermore . . .
  **--Dan Fogelberg, "Empty Cages" (Norbert Putnam,
  Michael Utley, and Russ Kunkel)**

"Brian, you've got to quit talking about Pauline. People don't want to hear about her anymore!"

These words were spoken by an active member of our congregation, who had asked me to stop by her home for a cup of coffee.

Blood rushed to my face. My stomach took a dive. I felt embarrassed, ashamed and angry! I felt violated!

I had just preached my second sermon since returning to Hemet, on October 3. I was beginning to find some hope, some light, but grief continued its strong hold. I didn't know how to write a sermon that wasn't, in some way, built around my loss. But I knew I had to try. So I had written that day's sermon in honor of the 800th anniversary of the birth of St. Francis of Assisi. I focused on his choosing of poverty (he had grown up in an affluent family), his humility, his love of nature and his work as a peacemaker.

In the sermon I talked about our calling to be peacemakers, and, since it was a Communion Sunday (we had communion only on the first Sunday of each month), I decided to end the sermon by proclaiming the way Holy Communion strengthens us to be peacemakers.

I never really understood the depths of this precious gift until Pauline and I shared it shortly before she died. When our life together was fast slipping away, this we could hold onto. When Pauline could no longer talk to me, this we could share, and this gift said everything that needed to be said.

As Pauline died she received life. The life that only Christ can give. Her Lord came to her, so simply, yet so profoundly. In his precious body and blood, he gave her life.

And I received new life. As Pauline died she gave me the only thing she could: her love, and her faith in our Savior. As she placed his body and blood in my mouth, I understood in a new way the greatest gift ever given us. On the edge of parting we never felt closer, bound together eternally by the love God gave us. Bound together sharing the most precious gift ever given, a gift for now, a gift for eternity.

Come to the Table of the Lord. Find in this simple gift the deepest truth. The truth about who you are. The truth about why you are here. The truth about what your mission in life is. We are the Body of Christ, and in his body we find our purpose, our fulfillment, our peace of mind and strength to be his people of peace in the world. Amen.

Now, three days later, this congregant was challenging me for talking about Pauline in my sermon. I asked her if she had heard my sermon. No, she hadn't, but others had told her about it. Defensively, I explained that I had tried intentionally to speak about something other than my loss, and, at the end of the sermon, had merely described how powerful Holy Communion had been for Pauline and me.

She said that that was still too much. I needed to stop talking about Pauline.

When I left I felt so alone, so misunderstood. I made my decision quickly. I would not talk about Pauline again publically. I would not share anything else that she had written. I would not share anything else that we had experienced. I would lock it all up. Tight. And I did. I didn't talk about Pauline for months.

I had experienced in an intensely painful way the feeling of violation so common in grieving: exposing something so precious and personal to you, and having it rejected by others. Long after others have heard enough, you still need to talk and share. When that sharing is rejected—through words, or even just a look—the pain is excruciating. That is why so many who grieve go behind closed doors with their pain long before the necessary healing has taken place.

That is why support groups, professional counseling and the rare friend or family member who will sit down with you, look you in the eyes, and say, "How are you really doing?" is so important in the grieving and healing process.

Violation is a form of a shaming experience. You expose yourself and it is rejected. As humans we respond to this with rage more so than anger. Anger is projected outwards. Rage is a turning inward as we raise up sturdy walls to protect ourselves. We decide not to let anyone else in as a way of protecting that which is most precious to us.

This creates in an obvious way a stumbling block when it comes to healing and wholeness. If healing comes by walking through grief with others, then anything that causes us to close in on ourselves and quit sharing our feelings hinders the healing process.

Fortunately for me, my turning in was not total. What I realized was that I had to be very careful where I shared my struggle. This, it is important to add, was not because there was anything wrong with Trinity Lutheran Church. In fact, overall, I am amazed at how the members of Trinity supported us through Pauline's illness and death and how many people kept reaching out to me after Pauline died. What I was learning (the hard way) was that, generally speaking, our culture does not know how to deal with death and grieving and we cannot assume that, just because we are choking on our pain, that everyone is ready and willing to "be there" for us.

It had been nearly three months since Pauline had died, and I was moving from pure lament to reflection on what I had experienced and learned. I reflected on how frequently I had been afraid and helpless in the face of Pauline's suffering. For so long I had carried the burden of wanting to protect Pauline from death, but knowing I could not. Now the fear was gone but the feeling of helplessness continued. I wrote: "This is the price one pays for love. When we enter into deep love we risk that feeling of helplessness, for we can never fully protect those we love—not from pain, not from rejection, not from fear, not from suffering, not from failure, not from death. Is it worth it? Of course it is! There is no question in my mind and heart about that. But there is no way around the feeling of helplessness. It is a painful journey. And I'm not home yet."

In the weeks after Pauline died, I kept reliving the painful events we had experienced. However, I was beginning to see beyond the pain and suffering to focus more clearly on the beauty of our ten years of marriage. I pictured her ill less often, and instead saw her shining face and beautiful smile as we walked hand-in-hand. I remembered holding each other as we drifted off to sleep. I pictured us sitting by the fireplace having long, intimate conversations.

People sometimes suggested that I begin to think about marrying again, but I felt no desire or need to. I was happy with the memory of our love and the feeling that we were still each other's. I wanted to remain faithful to Pauline, believing that could be enough for the rest of my life.

In mid-October I began teaching a Bible study on the book of Job, the most prominent book in the Bible on suffering, and God's relationship to that suffering. Perhaps through exploring Job's suffering and struggle to understand that suffering I would find some comfort.

Instead, I found myself thrust back into the throes of pain. Like Job, I longed for death, but it would not come [Job 3:21]: "Truly the thing that I fear comes upon me, and what I dread befalls me. I am not at ease, nor am I quiet; I have no rest; but trouble comes.'" [Job 3: 24-26, NRSV] This Bible study became another way of trying not to avoid my grief, but to move through it.

I also pushed myself back out into the world. Besides softball and tennis, I worked on my golf game, taking lessons from a professional instructor in Palm Springs. I attended synod events and retreats, one of them at a monastery where I came across a book by a priest, which led me to thinking of the priesthood notion of celibacy and marrying oneself to the church. Perhaps I could find meaning by remaining loyal to my marriage to Pauline, and throwing myself into working in the church. I also started to look into international ministry, working for peace and justice throughout the world. A mentor suggested I begin studying a foreign language and research organizations that place people overseas.

In the meantime, I was also considering a Doctor of Ministry degree. A friend from seminary suggested that I look into the program at Luther Seminary in St. Paul where we had received our Master of Divinity degrees. I hadn't thought of that possibility. His idea of going back to my midwestern roots intrigued me.

Finally I was beginning to look forward. I really needed this, for I was slowly dying by living in the past. In this, I had discovered another aspect of why I was surviving as well as I was. It was because of the purpose for which Pauline and I felt we were placed on this earth: to serve God; to be involved in the ministry and mission of the Body of Christ.

My life would have been entirely shattered if our goals in life had been to have a family, buy a house, accumulate beautiful possessions and a large estate. Then I would have nothing after losing Pauline. Instead Pauline strengthened me in striving to do God's will on this earth: to learn how to be merciful, compassionate and loving towards others; to feed the hungry; to liberate the oppressed; to share the Good News of Christ's redeeming love for all people. Pauline saw that as her purpose on earth and together we supported and helped each other become more committed to those values.

I was far from what I wanted to be, but the future Kingdom of God was luring me forward. It called me to go on and work for those goals Pauline and I valued. It gave me a reason to continue living, continue working, continue growing. I had a reason to live. I had a mission.

Pauline, thank you for your vision. You gave me not only love but also a deeper vision of our purpose on earth. Because of that love and vision I know my life is not over. For all the loneliness and emptiness I feel; for all the frustration and uncertainty; for all the weakness and feelings of powerlessness; in spite of all that I know there is a path for me to walk. Right now it is mainly uphill, but perhaps one day I will reach a plateau where I can again see clearly the glory of God.

Chapter 12   Good Friday: The Valley of Death

Across the vein of night
There cuts a path of searing light
Burning like a beacon
On the edges of our sight.
At the point of total darkness
And the lights divine divide
A soul can let its shadow stretch
And land on either side—
either side.
--Dan Fogelberg, "Nexus"

And at the ninth hour Jesus cried with a loud voice,

"E' lo-i, E'lo-i, lama sabach-tha'ni?" which means,
"My God, my God, why hast thou forsaken me?"
—Mark 15:34; RSV

"Brian, we really like your article and we plan to publish it this coming spring." It was the editor of "The Lutheran Standard" on the phone.

It was such a relief to hear that because sharing what Pauline had written to as wide a circle as possible was one of the few positive things that kept me going, especially now that I felt constrained when it came to talking about Pauline in my congregational setting.

As November arrived I began a six-week course in Riverside on Contemporary Theologies. I continued to teach the Job Bible Study, played softball and golf, spent many evenings with Chuck and kept being invited over to dinner by my wonderfully supportive friends.

I had started to feel somewhat more optimistic and hopeful, now three and a half months after Pauline's death. I had even recovered a bit of my sense of humor, although now it was more cynical. For example, one night Chuck and I drove past the cemetery where Pauline was buried on our way to the movies. As we passed by I rolled down the window of Chuck's car, and yelled out: "Pauline, I'm trying to be happy! I'm trying!"

Intense grief makes one so tired and weary that a part of you just wants relief, and the path to that appears to be positive thinking and a go-get-'em attitude. If you can just try a little harder you will be okay. This is what other people want you to do, and so why not just go out and do it.

Here's the problem. That is not going through the grief. It is attempting to go over or under or around it. And it doesn't work. But we think it will, and when it doesn't, we are sorely prepared for the plunge downward awaiting us.

Indeed, it would not take long for my newfound optimism to fall back into the abyss of lament, experiencing in some ways an even more difficult slide into pain and discouragement. This was the Good Friday Pauline had written about, which she knew I would go through. She had written that "it will be hell," which for me would become a great understatement.

There was a faint light at the end of the tunnel, but it was not the kind of light I wanted it to be. I wanted the light to be Pauline. The anguish of knowing that we would never be together again on this earth was paralyzing. One can do almost anything as long as there is hope of reunion. But when that hope has been destroyed, nothing really has any deep meaning

It is one thing to accept the fact that you can't have that which is essentially bad for you. It is something entirely different to accept that you can't have what is good for you, good for the world, and, yes, good for Pauline, for that is what she so desperately wanted. "At times the light is there. But it is so faint. And even when I see it, it can so quickly, like a candle in the wind, be snuffed out. 'Who will deliver me from this body of death,' as St. Paul put it? I want to say, 'Thanks be to God through Jesus Christ our Lord.' [Romans 7:24b-25a; RSV] But I can't; not yet."

The next day I poured out my soul again.

> It has been raining today. It has been cold and dark and wet. The chill in my body reflects the chill in my soul. I long for warmth but it isn't there. It can't be there. For the only one who can warm me lies deep beneath the earth—her body still, her body dead. I see her in her casket, deep beneath the earth. I see the rain pounding down on the earth above her and the wind howling around her. I see her body, stiff from death. I feel so sorry for her—there alone, beneath the earth, shivering in the cold. I want to hold her. I want to bring her in from the cold. Like the Carole King song, I want to say, "Come in from the rain, good old friend of mine."

> Yet I know Pauline is not cold. I am projecting. I am shivering in the rain, in the wind. I need to be warmed. I need to be invited in from the rain. I need somebody to warm me. But the one somebody who can really warm me is dead, cold, hidden beneath the earth, hidden by the reality of death, a reality which, like a concrete wall, walls in all my attempts to hold her again. I am crashing into that wall. I am crushed. I am severed. Severed from the heart that pumped the blood of life into my being.

> Oh, cold, windy, wet day. You do not hurt me. You just reflect the frozen state of my soul, of my spirit.

> Pauline's body is still and cold. But Pauline is not in that body. That is the reality of death. My body is warm and moving. I am in that body. But I feel cold and still, and dead. That is the reality of life, life in grief. That doesn't feel the way it should be. But that is the way I am.

I wanted to be positive, like I used to be. As I looked back through my journal entries, I saw a long line of negativity, pessimism, depression and despair. I searched deep in myself for some hope, and I forced myself to write hopefully. I hoped that once I began, I could continue to write about my healing. But let's admit what it was. I called it "Games Grieving People Play."

The old optimistic me wasn't there anymore. I tried to force myself to write what I wanted to feel, but it was just fantasizing. I didn't have anything new to say, or anything different.

> Let's simply and honestly state the verdict for the day: "No progress!" That's just the way it is, day after day after day. Nothing new. Nothing different. No healing. Just the same old grief, the same old pessimism, the same old depression and the same old sameness.
>
> I pity anyone who ever reads this. No new chapters. No new revelations. And certainly no climax, let alone a denouement.
>
> I believe this will not be forever. I guess that means I still have some hope. But right now it's hell.
>
> There! I wrote what I feel. Not what I want to feel. Not what others want me to feel. You know, I feel good about that. Not real good, but a little good. Some consolation! Interesting! Who's the cynic now?

The next day I took a more analytic approach, writing about where I was in my grief, so far as I could discern that, and what was now important to me in life. I talked about the meaning I had found in sharing Pauline's witness, especially now that I knew my article was going to be published, and I reflected on the possibility of writing a book based on more of her journal entries and our experience facing her death. But then it dawned on me that now I was writing about myself, which may have been therapeutic, but my laments contrasted so negatively with her faith and hope. As I put it, "Her witness is that of such a strong faith, a realistic and honest faith, in the face of death. Mine is hardly that. In the face of her death, to what am I witnessing?"

It then occurred to me that perhaps it was not a matter of a lack of faith. Pauline's strength was in being able to realistically admit her feelings about death. Perhaps what I was doing was realistically admitting my feelings about grief. Whether hope and faith were still there remained to be seen.

In that understanding I discovered another purpose for my writing: to be there for those who are grieving in the future. I put it this way: "I want to say to you: 'You are not alone. No matter where you are on the path of grief, regardless of how long it has been since the one you loved so dearly died, if you are still in despair, I say to you: You are not alone. I am there too. I have been there too.'"

I hoped that one day, when it did not hurt quite so much I would be able to look back from a stance of some healing without ever forgetting what it felt like to still be deep in the "valley of the shadow of death." [Psalm 23:4; RSV] I wanted to be able to use this experience to support others, to say,

> I was there, and I survived. Don't give up. Admit your despair, your depression, your agony, your grief, your cynicism. But don't give up.

> You and I are brothers, brother and sister. We have been through the Valley. We are in the Valley. But there is hope for coming out of the Valley. There is hope because God has promised there is hope. However faint that hope may seem, we must trust it. We have nothing else to trust. It is either suicide or trust. It is either nihilism or trust. It is either throwing our life away or trust. Hang in there. Don't give up. I

felt the way you do, but I made it through. I feel the way you do, but I am still alive.

Dear brother or sister in grief: Do not give up. Despair, but do not give up. Be angry, but do not give up. Be pessimistic, but do not give up. Be cynical, but do not give up. We are God's children. Because of that we dare trust and hope that meaning and purpose are never totally destroyed.

Chapter 13   Goodbye Yellow Brick Road

Man's youth is a wonderful thing:
It is so full of anguish and of magic
And he never comes to know it as it is,
Until it has gone from him forever.
--Thomas Wolfe

"We are so glad you could join us for Thanksgiving. Welcome!" Thanksgiving was at hand, and I had driven to Los Angeles to the home of brother, Paul, his wife, Susan, and their children, with Ansel and Dorothy joining us. It felt really good to be with family again

There comes a time in grief when the intensity begins to wear off, or at least lessens, and life becomes almost kind of blasé. It is the Saturday Pauline wrote about when she talked about the end of Holy Week as a microcosm of life. Held back less by the powerful Good Friday emotions of grief, one begins to move about a bit more freely, but without a lot of heart or feeling, as one becomes more reflective and tries to figure out what is next in life. As fall turned into winter, I told myself over and over again, "If I am still alive, then God must have a purpose for me, and I need to figure out now what that purpose is."

In the spirit of thanksgiving, I was beginning to find a sense of gratitude in my grieving: "I am thankful for many things. I thank you, God, for the precious gift of Pauline. You gave us undying, eternal love for each other, and that has given me all the happiness and fulfillment I need for a lifetime.

I thank you, God, for my family and friends. How precious they are. How understanding. How caring. I thank you for allowing me to bring your healing love to others. I also thank you for giving your healing love to me."

Returning home, I decided to send off a Christmas letter early, including two pages of quotations from Pauline's journal, and letting folks know they should watch "The Lutheran Standard" for the article about Pauline that would be appearing in May.

On a Sunday early in December I took the youth group to an immersion experience in Tijuana, Mexico, so that they could learn about the causes of poverty and hunger, and reflect on how we might respond to that suffering. On our way home, we stopped in San Diego for pizza, and I noticed that next door there was a large music store. The Lutheran radio producer had sent me a cassette tape of the program, called SCAN, that he had produced on Pauline's death and the importance of organ donation. He had paired the interview with powerful music written and sung by Dan Fogelberg. I wasn't familiar with his music, and so I walked into the music store to try to find the album from which the music came.

Finding the Fogelberg section, I thumbed through the albums. My heart nearly stopped! I had come to an album titled "The Innocent Age." On the cover was a female doll, in a long white dress, propped up against a gravestone. It looked like the dress in which Pauline had been buried.

Quickly I looked at the song titles. Yes, this had to be the album! I purchased it and that night, back at home, I played it. I heard all the music that John had selected. I found other pieces of music. It overpowered me. The tears flowed. How profoundly and beautifully Fogelberg had expressed many of my feelings of grief and loss! How well he had expressed the innocence that once was, but now was gone!

> Time stills the singing,
> A child holds so dear
> And I'm just beginning to hear
> Gone are the pathways

The child followed home
Gone, like the sand and the foam.
--Dan Fogelberg, "The Sand and the Foam"

The words made my mind soar. Images, pictures, memories, flooded my soul and spirit. I remembered Pauline in her hospital bed, two days before she died. I was talking about how cute she must have been as a child: pigtails and a carefree, loving spirit. I told her about myself as a child, and how sad I was that we grew up just 130 miles apart, but never knew each other in those early years. Here we were, both 31, on the precipice of being separated for the rest of my life on this earth, and now wishing we had been able to be together and share our love during those first 20 years we never knew each other.

Two weeks before, I had been on a retreat where we were led in a guided fantasy. The guide asked us to picture ourselves as children, and then picture an experience happening to us. I lay on the floor and remembered myself as an eight-year-old boy walking down the railroad tracks out of town, as I often did, bored, lonely, reflecting. Into that picture came Pauline as an eight-year-old. She walked up to me and we embraced. Embraced as two people who had always known each other, as two people meant to be together.

Then our leader said: "Frame that picture along with a strong, warm light coming into it." I saw the setting sun, strong in color as it slipped into the horizon, yet still giving forth warmth. In that picture I felt so secure, so warm, so loved.

He then told us to form a new picture, one of where we would be in two days. I saw myself on the eve of Thanksgiving, sitting on the couch at home, alone. Gone, like the sand and the foam. Gone now. Gone as long as I live.

Time stills the singing a child holds so dear. Oh God, where was my innocence? My dreams? Why couldn't we be together as children? Why can't we be together now? Why has that warm sun now set, leaving me cold, leaving me in darkness, leaving me alone?

The beauty of childhood is in being able to dream about what we have never had. But when one's dreams have come true, and then those dreams are shattered, how does one dream again? I lamented:

> I can't return to innocence. I can't dream about my dear love coming to me, because she has already been here. And now she is gone. God, are my dreams over? How can I look forward when all I want to do is go back? Where is Pauline? Where is my mom? Oh, Mother God, take me in your arms and hold me, soothe me, wipe away my tears, tell me it will be okay. Suffer your little child to come unto you, and hold me, just hold me. I need to be held so badly. Oh, Pauline, my little pig-tailed Pauline! Whatever happened to our dreams?"

I kept myself busy with many pre-Christmas church activities and with sports. I went skiing one day at Snow Valley, and then returned to golf, proving you can do both on the same day in parts of California. In the middle of the month our softball team won our division championship. The last play of the final game was a smash to me at third base. I caught it, decided to keep the ball, and started jumping for joy as all of us congratulated one another. I was surprised that I could feel so happy about anything, let alone winning a softball game. I felt real joy as we headed out for pizza to celebrate. Maybe I was finally beginning to throw myself back into life.

Before Pauline died, I had really struggled with the relationship of suffering to God's will, and concluded that God was not causing her suffering. I thus wondered if, after her death, I would feel close to God in a way that I hadn't after Mom's and Dad's deaths.

I found that apart from my memories of Pauline, there was nothing that moved me more than the tears of others. Not their words, not their touch, but their tears. That look of caring helplessness, wanting so much to do something, but knowing there is nothing that can be done. The most meaningful gift others gave me in my grieving, and gave Pauline through the experience of dying, was their tears. Nothing demonstrates greater love, greater sensitivity, greater compassion, greater understanding.

I knew that God, too, was crying with me. God felt my pain, as God feels the pain and suffering of all God's helpless children: the grieving, the suffering, the hungry, the ill, the oppressed. God's tears flow to the earth, mingle with our tears, and create a river of passionate love that cleanses and gives new life to all who will allow their tears to fall into that stream.

"I must find courage in those tears. I will find courage in those tears. In the tears of God, in the tears of others," I wrote. As long as we can care enough about each other to cry for each other, we will find a way to go on. Our tears, sacramentally mingling with God's tears, will carry us forward, buoying us up through pain and suffering, strengthening us to bring love and justice where we can, cleansing us of the frustration and hopelessness we often feel, until, one day, we arrive together downstream at the Kingdom of God. There God will wipe away every tear from our eyes, and there will be no more sorrow. "But until that day, we must continue to love, we must continue to trust, we must continue to care, we must continue to hope, we must continue to cry."

On December 29, Mom's and Neil's birthdays, and my parents' anniversary, I boarded a plane to fly to Minneapolis for the annual Convocation at Luther Seminary, along with the five-year reunion banquet of my graduating class.

I felt amazingly relaxed and somewhat secure. I was gong back to the womb. Home country.

I would be glad to see 1982 end. It had been a year of fear and anxiety, a year in which my worst nightmares became a reality. It was still a good year as long as Pauline was alive, but from July 13 onward it was truly a nightmare.

Before going to the airport, I had stopped by Pauline's grave. As usual I spoke of what had recently transpired, how I was feeling and what I was planning for the future. As I prepared to leave, saying that this would be the last time I would be by her side in 1982, a painful thought came to me. "Honey," I said, "this year I won't be able to kiss you at midnight on New Year's Eve." The tears began to slowly fill my eyes. Quietly I stood there, absorbed by a feeling of emptiness, a feeling of deep sadness.

I returned to my car and drove home. The tears dried. I packed and drove to San Diego. A strange peace came over me. A feeling of anticipation grew within me.

I could no longer live in the past as much as I had been. I had to begin to look toward the future. It wasn't what I wanted, but this is the way it was. 1982 was soon gone. Pauline was gone.

> Pauline, I don't want to let you go. But I must. Like walking away from your grave, I must walk away from you. Not because I want to, but because I have to. Like a butterfly about to break open its cocoon, I must break open a new life. I want to remain in the cocoon, but I am being thrust out of it. That thrust is painful, but it is the only way I can survive.
>
> Goodbye 1982. Goodbye Pauline. I must leave you. But I will never forget you. Never, ever. I need your love. I need the courage you had. But that courage must now be not so much the courage to face the past as courage to live into the future.
>
> Pauline, I love you so much. Goodbye, my love. Goodbye. Goodbye.

While in St. Paul, I was interviewed for a Lutheran television series on death and dying. From St. Paul I flew to Bismarck to visit brother Alan and Pauline's parents.

In January I flew back to San Diego. I was headed home but it felt like I was leaving home. St. Paul and the seminary were filled with so many memories of Pauline and our life together there.

I was in transition from my past into a new and unknown future. I knew I would make it, somehow, and I no longer wanted to die. But I still wasn't thrilled about living. I was not as empty, but I was still so far from being filled.

> I am leaving home. And I want to leave, in a way. I have to leave. I can't stand to go on and on living in the pain of the past. In a way my tears today were not so much in regards to the past itself as to the act of having to leave it. It's so painful to say goodbye Pauline. Goodbye my love. How can I leave what was so precious to me? But I must in order to live again. I must. God, it hurts so badly. It hurts so deeply to leave what I don't want to leave, but what I must leave.

> I remember looking deep into Pauline's eyes before her last cardiac arrest. "Goodbye," she said with her eyes. "Goodbye," I said. Goodbye my love. Goodbye my honey. Goodbye my darling. Now I say goodbye again. Goodbye Pauline. Goodbye Bismarck. Goodbye our dreams. Goodbye our hopes. Goodbye. Goodbye. Goodbye.

Chapter 14   The Winter of My Spirituality: Rebirth, Yet Again

Silent sea
Tell this to me:
Where are the children we used to be?

Silent sea:
At picture shows
Where nobody goes
And only the heart can see.

Starry skies
Soft lullabies
Where do they go when their melodies die?

Starry skies:
To a day
Far, far away
That only the heart may know.

Friends we knew
Follow us through
All of the days of our lives.
Love we shared
Waits for us there
Where our wishes forever reside.

Falling tears
Memories' mirrors
Where are the summers
Oh, where are the years?

Falling tears:
Carried far

To a wandering star
That only the heart can know.
--Dan Fogelberg, "Only the Heart May Know"

"How wicked it would be, if we could, to call the dead back!" These words, written by C.S. Lewis in his book [A Grief Observed] about the death of his beloved wife, Joy, hit me like a bolt of lightning.

Marriage is a strange institution. It demands lifelong fidelity, which rightly scares most of us as we contemplate whether we can live up to such all-encompassing vows. Then, when we finally gather the courage to make that challenging commitment, we often discover joy beyond what we could ever have imagined. Furthermore, when death comes, and we have fulfilled our vows, we no longer know how to move on. Our vow was until "death us do part," but we may find ourselves committed far beyond that, not just until the death of our beloved, but also until our own death.

This is where I found myself, in a kind of purgatory, knowing I needed to leave the past, but still not ready to embrace the future fully.

I was entering the **winter** of my spirituality, or what the scriptures call the **desert** or **wilderness**. The intense emotion had begun to subside somewhat--although I never knew when it might rear its ugly head once again—leaving me in a time of cold, loneliness and darkness, to use the winter metaphor, or a time of emptiness, thirst and abandonment, to use the desert metaphor. In the spiritual journey you never arrive at mountaintop experiences of revelation and insight until you have first gone through the desert experience of purgation.

The winter of faith is also a time of struggle between the will and the heart. In grief the will often speeds ahead of the heart. We come to the point where we know we need to get better, where we want to get better, where we write and talk about getting better, where we may even think we are getting better. This is an essential step, although not an easy one, because winter has a way of freezing us into stasis and inaction, with our heart refusing to go where our mind and will are trying to take us.

Now, back at home from my reflective trip, I fell again into the painfulness of an empty heart. Martin Marty calls it the "cry of absence," or a "wintery kind of spirituality." Others call it the "dark night of the soul." Whatever you call it, I felt it. An ache so deep, so strange, so penetrating. Like a body surfer trying to catch a wave, racing towards the shore, the wave broke, and I came crashing into the rocks and sand.

Who can understand the strange movements of the human spirit? Who can understand the paradoxical feelings deep within? Who can understand the movement between pain and healing, doubt and faith, despair and hope?

The reason I kept crying became harder and harder to pinpoint. There was such a deep restlessness in my soul, such a deep uneasiness. My pain was a confusion of grief over the past and fear of the future. I wanted to step into the future, but I was afraid of doing so alone. I was afraid to chart my future without Pauline to give me support and guidance.

The pain came less often. Sometimes I went two or three weeks without weeping, but when it did come, it was every bit as excruciating as on the day Pauline died.

I needed to be held yet I could not reach out. But the phone never rang. So I sat alone in my fear, feeling a sorrow so deep and pervasive that it was beyond expression. This was the "dark night of the soul" St. John of the Cross wrote about. It was night, but too early to sleep. The sun was setting, orange and yellow, the colors of hope, yet I felt no hope. All I felt was the darkness enveloping me. A darkness I couldn't explain. But I could feel it. I sat alone in that darkness, crying for the emptiness, the absence, in my life.

Into the dark night of my soul came Chuck. He was the friend with whom I could fully share myself. He listened and talked, laughed and cried with me. I told him about my trip home, and I read to him my last three journal entries. As I shared and we talked, my feelings became clearer and clearer.

Chuck put into words what I could not: I felt both frustration regarding the progress I had not made yet, and a strange kind of uneasiness regarding what progress I had made. Most of what I had been feeling in that period had to do with the latter.

I felt uneasy about moving into my new future. I felt uneasy about leaving my past life behind. I did not feel guilty. Pauline made so many efforts in conversation and in her writing to set me free from that, and to encourage me to move ahead as best I could without guilt. But I felt unfaithful. I had so committed my life to her, and built it around her, that I felt a kind of unfaithfulness as I made enough progress in my grieving to begin to try to move ahead without her.

Even as I faced the fear of a future without her, deep down I felt uneasy about it. I had said goodbye with my lips, but my heart wanted to hang on. I walked away with my feet, but tears came forth drawing me back. This was my transition, between past and future, between total faithfulness to Pauline and being forced to move ahead without her. A transition between total love for Pauline, and knowing I must now give that love to others. Like an infant about to be born, I was being pushed into a new world, a new world I wanted and needed, but a world that meant I must leave the security and happiness of the womb. Even after Pauline died, I still found security and comfort in the world we created together. As I grieved and cried and lamented our separation, I found my meaning and being in reference to her and our life together. I found my meaning in memories, in the past.

Now I had to leave an entire way of life built around her. To leave that way of life was no more unfaithful to her than the infant's birth is unfaithful to his/her mother. So my head told me. So Pauline told me. But my heart was not yet in tune with my head.

But thanks to Chuck, I better understood where I was and I began to feel I could live with that ambiguity of my transition

I knew there were many dark nights ahead of me and many strange feelings to experience and understand. But through the tears, through the writing, through sharing with my friends, I would find a way through:

> Thank you, Pauline. You walked so many steps with me. Then you had to go on ahead of me. But you showed me the way with courage, faith, hope and such gracious love. I will go on now without you, only and simply because I must, just as you had no choice about gong on without me. But I will never forget you. You will always be a part of my life, and I will always feel your absence in my heart and being. Pauline, thank you for holding onto me, and letting me hold onto you, as long as we could. And for telling me to let go when the time came for me to try to truly live again.

> Thank you, God. Thank you for the boundless love you have shown me; for the everlasting love Pauline gave me, for the support and unconditional love of so many friends; for a heart that can feel, for eyes that can cry. And thank you for the light that inevitably comes to bathe in warmth and beauty the dark night of the soul.

In addition to reading Martin Marty's book, A Cry of Absence, written after the death of his wife, I also read C.S. Lewis' book about the death of his wife, Joy, which ends with these words: "How wicked it would be, if we could, to call the dead back! She [Joy] said not to me but to the chaplain, 'I am at peace with God.' She smiled, but not at me."

I had always seen the "going ahead" of those who have died as negative. No doubt this is because of the fears of death we all harbor when we are not near it, and because I knew Pauline wanted to live so desperately. But in the end, I'm not sure that Pauline really demonstrated any great fear for herself. Her fear was feeling that she had to continue to be strong for me. And as I think back even further, I don't recall her ever talking about being afraid of death for herself, but rather how miserable she knew I would be once she died. This was no conceit on her part: I made it plenty clear over and over again how afraid I was of having to live without her.

In fact, a friend of Pauline's told me of a conversation she had with her in April:

> Pauline: Have you ever thought about death?
> Friend: Yes, I have. Have you?
> Pauline: Yes.
> Friend: Are you afraid to die?
> Pauline: No, I'm not. But I don't want to leave Bear. However, I think I am going home soon.

As I pictured Pauline's last hours, even between all those cardiac arrests, I didn't remember fear. Pain, yes; agony, yes; gasping for air, yes; but not fear. I was the one weeping as I gave her communion. Her response was to muster all her energy to reach up and embrace me. And she smiled at me so often those last hours, even right before she died. As I think about it, it was like she was trying to comfort and console me as best she could.

And why did she keep coming back to life? Was it really for herself? I suppose to a point it was, at least as long as she thought there was hope of a transplant. But did she really believe there was still hope? Wasn't her body telling her she was dying? About that I'm not sure. I think it did tell her that, indeed, she was dying, but Pauline still gallantly refused to give up hope until I had to tell her it was hopeless. Whatever, could it be that a large part of why she kept coming back was for me? Because she knew how much I needed her? Because she wanted to keep consoling me as long as she could?

After all, Pauline had had two out-of-body experiences. And she had told me they were positive. Why would she want to keep coming back into such a broken body that was filled with pain and agony?

I know I was afraid. And I guess I had assumed she was, too. But was she? I think it is quite possible, even plausible, that she wasn't.

Those who die go ahead of us. Do we assume that the road ahead for them is so painful and fearsome because we who remain are projecting the fears we feel in being left behind? Is our desire for our dead loved ones to return strictly selfish, because our lives are so painful without them? Is death only fearsome when we are not yet at its door? Can there be peace and serenity and acceptance at that door?

Pauline wrote that in her solitude she was becoming more in tune with God. She wrote about dying with a deep spirituality. She said God's tears were enough. She died with a respirator lodged in her throat. Pauline could not speak the words, "I am at peace with God." But her eyes said it.

In the end, it was I who was not at peace, who was afraid, who still had to walk the journey to the threshold of the door of death, without Pauline by my side. Pauline had already done that. And done it so well.

Yes, C.S. Lewis was right: it would be strictly selfish to call our dead loved ones back to this life.

As I found a way to begin to let Pauline go, I was also finding a way to move more positively into the future. I contacted both Claremont University in Los Angeles and Luther Seminary in St. Paul about their Doctor of Ministry programs. I also did not find myself going to Pauline's grave nearly as often, and I went over a month without writing in my journal.

Healing, although slow, was beginning to show itself. When I looked at Pauline's pictures, the pain didn't feel as deep. In fact, I felt a strange kind of satisfaction and comfort in knowing how deeply we loved, how deeply we cared. I was proud of the fact that we were married and grateful for the time we had together. I was able to look back with more peace and less pain. I was able to be thankful for what we had together, and think less about what we had lost.

Pauline was still with me and would always be part of my life. I no longer needed to look at her pictures, visit her grave, read her journal, or listen to our songs as often as I once had. I didn't need those things as much to "feel" her, to "remember" her. All the memories and feelings had filtered down into a kind of unity of her in me.

I was not through the winter yet, though. One battleground leads to another. First I had to battle grief. Now I was battling apathy. The problem, however, was that I was not really battling. I was so drained, so used up, so spent; there just wasn't much to me anymore. I had wanted to feel less pain and emptiness and grief but now I just wanted feel anything, to care again. I wanted something to really make a difference to me. How ironic that Pauline died needing a new heart and now I was not living because my heart died with her.

"Lord," I prayed, "deep down inside I'm trying to muster some energy. Some feeling. And about all I can come up with is this: 'God, don't let me die before I am dead. Heal me more deeply. Let this broken, cracked heart begin to pump the blood of new life again.' I guess for now I'll have to be content with hope as a thought in the mind. It certainly isn't a feeling in the heart."

I slowly accepted that I could not continue to give all my love to Pauline. That would be living in the past, living in memories. To go on and on giving all your love to someone who has died is to begin to die yourself. And I needed to live. I had to find a way to love and give more of myself to the people around me, the people among whom I worked. Slowly I was beginning to realize and accept that Pauline had found her new life, and now I needed to find mine.

In February, at our Ash Wednesday service, I placed ashes on the forehead of each worshipper, saying over and over, "Remember that you are dust, and to dust you shall return."

I was moved by the words. So much came into perspective. Pauline's experience was not unique. We are all from the dust, and to the dust we all shall return. I felt such a deep feeling of honesty and reality in reminding each person of that, and in being reminded of that myself. I felt cleansed and freed to live.

As I looked out at the congregation, I remembered that Pauline's last worship service had been Ash Wednesday the year before. How appropriate. How significant.

I felt a deep satisfaction in knowing that what she went through, what we went through, was a journey of faith, accompanied every step of the way by one who also suffered, one who also knew pain, separation, fear, loneliness, death.

Two days later I took our youth group up into the San Jacinto Mountains for a weekend retreat. Near the end of the retreat I asked each participant to write a letter to themselves, seal it, address it to themselves, and I would take the letters and mail them back in six months. I wrote one to myself:

> Dear Bear, Dear Brian,
>
> You are two people: a Bear of the past; a new Brian trying to find a new future. As you wrote on Valentine's Day, Pauline has found her new life, and now you must find yours.
>
> Bear, let the past go. You have beautiful memories, and Pauline's love forever. But now you must move on.
>
> Brian, trust yourself to God. Trust the future. You will be fulfilled if you focus on what is most important in life: your spirituality—being open and honest before God, getting in touch with the pain of the world and giving of yourself in love to others.
>
> You must find your security in God, and begin to fully share yourself with others. Yes, one day you may again be in love, but that cannot be the basis on which to now build your entire future. That would only lead to frustration, uncertainty and continuing unhappiness.

The task is quite clear. You must let yourself go deep into spirituality--prayer, solitude, reading, loving, and sharing of your being with others.

I concluded the letter with a prayer:

"Lord, make me an instrument of your peace." Fill me with your love and the deep inner peace that only you can give. Lead me to reach out to others in genuine compassion and love, receiving others even as you receive them. Let your grace fill my life and radiate out in all my relationships. Lead me in the paths of righteousness for your name's sake. [Psalm 23:3] Wherever I go, Lord, let me walk each step as your child. Love, Brian

Chapter 15   Show Me the Way to Love

Sometimes in the night I feel it
Near as my next breath, and yet, untouchable
Silently the past comes stealing
Like the taste of some forbidden sweet

Every ghost that calls upon us
Brings another measure in the mystery
Death is there
To keep us honest
And constantly remind us we are free

Down the ancient corridors
And through the gates of time
Run the ghosts of days
That we left behind
--Dan Fogelberg, "Ghosts"

"We are writing to inform you that you have been accepted into our Doctor of Ministry program, effective this fall, 1983." Arriving in late February, the letter was from the admission's committee at the School of Theology at Claremont. I was given until March18 to decide if I wanted to enter their program.

One of the strange things about the journey of grief is the extremes. There are times when you don't even know if you want to keep on living, as when I would go to Pauline's grave and feel like laying down beside her and pulling the earth over both of us.

Then there are times, as you are trying to open yourself to the future, when you almost feel normal as you struggle with the realities and decisions of life.

The letter from Claremont was one of those times. While excited to receive it, it also created a struggle within me. I was leaning towards going back to the bosom of the Midwest, but I had not yet heard from the admissions committee at Luther Seminary. Furthermore, the particular program I wanted to enter, Ministry is Pastoral Care and Social Change, had no other applicants. It was not certain that the program would even be offered.

When the March 18 deadline arrived, I had still not heard from Luther Seminary, but couldn't shake the need to return to my roots. I wrote Claremont thanking them for the opportunity, but declining the invitation.

It was good to finally be able to plan for and think about the future, even with all the uncertainties—not that this growing positivity was a straight line. I continued to have a variety of emotional experiences, from grief to anger to emptiness. Like a decayed tooth in an otherwise healthy body, the pain would come from time to time, pointing to a problem that sooner or later had to be confronted. But, unlike a decayed tooth, I couldn't pinpoint what the problem was.

I had certainly made a great deal of progress. I had come a long way. Yet something extremely important was still lacking. I felt I was operating too much out of weakness rather than strength. But I wasn't even sure what that meant.

I took a four-day vacation a couple of weeks after Easter, thinking this would help, but, as soon as I returned home, it was clear that it had made little difference. I was still really struggling to move ahead with my life.

One morning, after a restless night's sleep, I awoke with a sense of new insight, a dawning revelation. I finally began to realize that the weakness I was operating out of was the trying to control what I could not control. I was allowing everyone and everything around me to determine how I felt and thus needed to control outcomes of events in order to ensure my own happiness. I wanted life to give me a break, but there was no way to guarantee that. I knew that pain, could follow pain, could follow pain.

This was my weakness. I had no inner strength. Like a sponge, I was at the mercy of having to absorb whatever flowed my way, whether wine or vinegar. I was lacking a deep spirituality and awareness of my call. I was weak in body, weak in spirit, and, therefore, weak psychologically.

I bolted out of bed, put on running clothes, and ran in the cool air until I was tired. When I came home, I listened to music and read scripture and books on spiritualty, reflecting and praying on what I was reading and hearing. Then, with cracking voice that had not awakened yet to the day, I picked out a song and began to play guitar and sing. Again, I turned on the music, and listened as I finished preparing to go to work.

I heard from John Michael Talbot the words I needed to hear. He was singing a song based on Psalm 62:

> Only in God is my soul at rest,
>   In Him comes my salvation.
> He only is my rock,
>   my strength and my salvation.
> My stronghold, my Savior,
>   I shall not be afraid at all.
> My stronghold, my Savior,
>   I shall not be moved.
>
> Only in God is found safety,
>   When enemy pursues me.
> Only in God is found glory,
>   When I am found weak and found lowly.
>
> My stronghold, my Savior,
>   I shall not be afraid at all.
> My stronghold, my Savior,
>   I shall not be moved.
>
> Only in God is my soul at rest,
>   In Him comes my salvation.
> **--John Michael Talbot, "Psalm 62"**

That day I entered the office with a new sense of life. I felt closer to God. I felt relaxed, and open to those around me, ready to carry on whatever work needed to be done.

Each day I continued the same routine and each day I became more aware of the beauty of life, more present to others, more able to trust myself to God. A week earlier I had cried out, "My God, when will the pain ever end?" Now I had received an answer: "Pain will always be there. It will never end. But I will give you the strength to bear it, to use it, to grow through it."

I had wondered if my new theology--that God did not cause Pauline's suffering and death--would lead me to feel closer to God than I had after the deaths of Mom and Dad. It had indeed. But now I was going a step further. I was not only able to pray to God, to feel close to God, but to rely on God to uplift and carry me regardless of what happened next in my day, or in my life. Having lost the people most important to me, I now turned myself over to God more fully than ever before. Rather than continually lament what I had lost, I was slowly beginning to open myself to the beauty of the world still before me, my place in that world, my new calling in that world.

I continued to pour myself into work as best I could. I taught a course on the prophet Jeremiah, focusing on the ways he struggled with his call to prophetically announce the ways of the kingdom of God.

Moved by my trip with the youth to Mexico, I taught a course entitled "Faith, Love, and Justice," and out of that class formed a Hunger Action Committee to work on ways to overcome hunger in the world. In addition, in April the youth group participated in a 30 hour overnight fast to raise money for world hunger.

By the April Church Council meeting, I had made my major decisions. The program at Luther Seminary had enough students registered so I resigned my call effective June 1 to move back to St. Paul and enter the Ministry in Pastoral Care and Social Change program as a first step in a Doctor of Ministry degree.

Telling the council my plans to leave was difficult and very emotional. I had not really planned how my announcement would end, but the words just flowed forth: "When you interviewed me, Pauline and I were in a desperate situation. You could have easily turned away from us, but you received us with warmth and love, and gave us the chance for the only hope we had. You have continued to support and love me. When I think of Hemet I will always think of much pain. But I also will remember how you walked with us into the Valley of the shadow. I'm not out of the Valley yet, but I have come a long way. And when the day comes that I am 'on the road again,' I will continue to remember all of you who helped me get there by walking through the Valley with me."

How good it was to want to live and love again, to have hope, and to be able to feel trust. No matter what the future held, I trusted that God had a purpose for my life.

God had been so patient with me and now I had to be patient with myself. Like a fawn newly born, I felt ready to run straight away into the meadows of my new life, even if my legs were still wobbly. I knew that I would stagger and fall, but Mother God would pick me up and nurse my wounds.

As long as we live and love, we will experience grief over the loss of those we want to be close to, and cannot. Once one understands that grief never ends, then it doesn't matter so much where one is in the grieving process. What does matter is that one begins to find a reason to live again, to love again.

I promised to myself that, although I would continue to shed many tears for Pauline and for others I had lost and would lose, those tears would not simply carry me back into the past but would become a river that carried me into the future. They would remind me of how much I have been loved, how much I have loved, and that I was called to continue to love and be loved as long as there is breath within me.

The next weeks were difficult. Saying goodbye to so many people who had truly touched my life, and helped carry me on my journey out of the valley, brought more pain, more grief. Like Pauline, I wanted them to know how much I appreciated their love. Even so, I was ready to move on to the next stage of my journey.

John Michael Talbot's lyrics once again captured my feelings:

My God, and my all,
I should like to love you,
And give you my heart,
And give you my soul.
And so I will yearn for you,
In the depths of your passion,
Show me the way to love,
Show me the way to give my life for you.

Show me the way to love,
Then we will surely rise,
To fly like an eagle, through the wind,
To find in your dying, Lord,
We both shall live again. So fly . . . . .

So I will weep with you,
In the depth of your passion,
I will not be ashamed,
To travel the world,
Weeping out loud for love,
Show me the way to love,
Show me the way to love,
Then we will surely rise.
--"My God and My All"

On May 6, our wedding anniversary, the article I wrote about Pauline, entitled "With All My Heart," appeared in "The Lutheran Standard" Within days I received letters from all around the country: from the Bishop and Bishop Emeritus of the American Lutheran Church, classmates in seminary, former parishioners and many pastors and laypeople I had never met. I was very moved by the responses I received.

Many people told of the tears they shed as they read the article, and how much they were affected by Pauline's faith.

Typical of the responses I received was a letter from a classmate serving a parish in Minnesota: "I had not realized Pauline had died until I read the story. The courage, depth of feeling, honesty, and true humanity reflected there, combined, for me, to form a powerful witness to love and faith."

A woman from Minnesota, whose husband had died, thanked me for sharing Pauline's journal: "Many of us do not have those treasures of our loved ones—we must depend on memories. Your wife prayed to live long enough to touch people's lives—in death, with your written word—she is doing that."

A pastor in Wisconsin I had never met wrote: "It is possible that I have read words as powerful as those in your article, 'With All My Heart' before, but I don't remember where they could have come from. It seems impossible that so few words could affect me so deeply. I am not sure what the effect of those words will be on my life, but I know I have glimpsed something special."

The publication of the article was one more piece of closure I needed as I prepared to leave Hemet.

In my farewell sermon later that month, I shared:

I remember writing in my journal one day last fall: "First Dad, then Mom, now Pauline. How do I go on living without the presence of the three most important people in my life?"

I still struggle with their absence, and the pain of it, and I always will. But slowly I have come to realize a truth: not only do we not possess even those closest to us, but, no matter what our circumstance in life, the voids we all have in our lives can only be filled, in any lasting sense, by the love of God.

In other words, my journey these past months has not only been a psychological journey of grief, but also a spiritual journey of finding a renewed faith, renewed hope, renewed peace.

It has not been easy for me to learn how to "let go" of Pauline, but I have come a long way. I am grateful to you, and I always will be, for you have helped me in so many ways to believe that my life still has a purpose. You have not been afraid to stand by me in my sorrow, and support me through the "Valley of the shadow." [Psalm 23:4]

It is also not easy for me to let you go, but now is my time to do that. As I do, I pray that God will continue to fill you with God's love so that you may experience joy in the "now," hope even when the "now" is painful, and trust in God's promise that our lives will only be fulfilled as long as we strive to serve our Lord.

The congregation then ushered me outside and planted a tree in honor and memory of Pauline.

Within a few days I would wave goodbye to the San Jacinto Valley and head back to the Midwest to spend the summer with my brother, Alan, in Bismarck. Upon my arrival, my college roommate, Joel, called to say that his church was without a pastor. They needed a part-time interim pastor. I accepted the invitation.

I led services at the Church of the Cross on June 12 and immediately felt excited about being a part of this congregation for the summer. Even though this wasn't Pauline's parents' church, they attended whenever I led worship. They also invited me to dinner several times over the summer. It was very meaningful to spend time with them again, to have the opportunity to be in Pauline's childhood home where we had spent so much time early in our marriage, to see belongings of Pauline's that she had left there. There were plenty of tears, but also a growing sense of gratitude for what Pauline and I had experienced together.

That summer, I went on a travel seminar to Germany and Austria. While there, we visited the concentration camp at Dachau. Walking through the barbed-wire fences, entering the barracks crammed with wooden bunks, seeing the cremation ovens, I wept. How great is the suffering of the world! How much agony and grief were created in this place!

Chapter 16 Easter: Lo, I Am With You Always

My Lord God, I have no idea where I am going. I do not see the road ahead of me. I cannot know for certain where it will end. Nor do I really know myself, and the fact that I think I am following your will does not mean that I am actually doing so. But I believe the desire to please you does in fact please you. And I hope I have that desire in all that I am doing. I hope that I will never do anything apart from that desire. And I know that if I do this you will lead me by the right road, though I may know nothing about it. Therefore I will trust you always though I may seem to be lost and in the shadow of death. I will not fear, for you are ever with me, and you will never leave me to face my perils alone.

--Thomas Merton, "Thoughts in Solitude"

"Sunday, Bear, you will be happy. You will always miss me, but that does not mean missing out on life." Pauline's words came to me often as the summer wore on. I had come a long way in my grief journey, but was I anywhere near Sunday yet? Was I ready to get back into life again?

I looked with mixed feelings toward the date, July 13, which would be one year since Pauline had died. It has become common wisdom that if you can just make it through the first year of grieving, things will automatically improve. I wondered if that would be the case for me.

So, what is it about one year? I didn't know if I would feel relief that finally that first year was over, or, if I would be afraid to let that year go. I found it hard to believe that there is any kind of magic about one year, and yet, I had to admit that I was much better. But was it real healing? I am always amazed at our endless ability to keep questioning ourselves, including progress we may have made.

The grief journey is strange in that way. You get to the point where you are able to relax and lay back, floating gently on the water, but you keep wondering if something will reach up and pull you under.

Even though I was functioning much better and actually finding ways to enjoy life again, I continued to feel a pervading sense of sadness. The intense pain had subsided, but a veneer of sadness remained. I wondered what that was all about.

Reflecting on this, it seemed that the further I got away from Pauline's death and the more I healed, the more I realized just how sad it is to leave what you don't want to leave. The plain, simple, clear fact was that I didn't like living my life without Pauline. No matter how much I learned to live without her and to be comfortable in my solitude and aloneness, the truth was that I was learning how to live a life that I did not choose. I had accepted the fact of this new life, but I didn't like it. I wanted to grow old with Pauline, walking through life together, holding hands, until our hands were wrinkled and old. I wondered how deep my happiness could ever be again. I wondered if I was destined—for the rest of my life—to live a "half-hearted" life?

It was like holding a small bird in your hands. You know you can't hold it forever; you have to let it go. So you slowly begin to lighten your grasp. However, you find it so difficult to take the last step, and open your hands wide enough for the bird to actually fly away.

What makes that final letting go so difficult? It is the reality that you are being forced to accept that which you do not want to accept: that the person you love so much is really gone, and is not coming back.

No matter how you cut it, death is not a problem to be solved. It stares you in the face and refuses to move. It separates you from those you love and need and never gives them back. You make it through the first year, but, unlike serving a sentence in prison, you are not reunited with those you love. You serve the sentence, and when you walk outside the jailhouse fence, you find yourself standing alone. The air is cool, the sun shines brightly, old friends are there to greet you, but you still feel alone. Alone, because those you love most remain gone. There will be new friendships, and there may be new loves, but a part of you remains gone, a part of your heart forever unable to move into the future because it refuses to forget and let go of its commitment to those you once loved "with all your heart. Always have. Always will."

How much death can we take? I guess we each have to answer that for ourselves. Some have lost their whole families in the fires of Dachau, and survived, and even survived well. Others lose a spouse and never live again. I believe the key to survival is to admit frankly that death forever changes us. That death leaves holes in our hearts that will never fully heal. We die if we naively cling to the notion that one day we will be totally healed, that one day we will again be as happy as we once were.

We can be happy again, but it will be different. Perhaps the greatest enemy is the attraction of absorbing ourselves in contemplation of a fantasy world of innocence and naïveté'. Life changes us in ways that move us forever beyond innocence. We know that clearly about sin and guilt. It is also true of death. I may think back to playing catch with Dad, laying with my head on Mom's lap, or walking hand-in-hand with Pauline on a beautiful fall evening, but all that can never be again. To live again is not to return to the past, but to move into the future honestly admitting the pain we carry, accepting the way we have been changed.

The next sacred event on my calendar was Pauline's birthday, July 25. As I sat down to write, I soon realized that my tears were less for my loss and more a reflection of the unbelievable beauty, love and grace that continued in my life:

> The journey into the Valley of the Shadow is a journey of grace. We dare go into the Valley because our lives are a gift, our loved ones are a gift, and our hope for courage and strength comes not from ourselves, but from our God. And if we are to come

out of that Valley of the Shadow we will do so only in grace; the grace of God, the grace of those waiting to care for us.

My tears are less and less for Pauline. My tears are less and less for me. My tears are more and more borne out of the realization of just how gracious our lives are, how blessed we are, in the midst of our sorrow, to have a Lord and so many people who really do care. Less and less my tears are a reflection of loneliness and self-pity and sorrow over Pauline's suffering, and more and more a reflection of the joy and blessedness of a life in which we are constantly offered the love of God and the caring companionship of so many willing to share our burdens and our pain.

The worst thing we can do with our lives is to live in denial, refusing to recognize our own pain and the pain of those around us. Such life may appear smooth sailing on the surface, but because it is lived on the surface there is no deep joy and no deep passion. It is like a plant with no root or a sailboat with no centerboard. The second worst thing we can do with our lives—once we have recognized our pain—is to refuse to ever come out of it, to refuse to live again. Wallowing in our pain endlessly turns the compassion and sympathy of others into pity and theologically is a refusal of grace.

In mid-August I moved to the Twin Cities and visited the ministry sites that would be a part of my Doctor of Ministry studies. My excitement really began to grow as I anticipated beginning studies and working in a local congregation and at the Center for Global Education at Augsburg College.

Returning to Bismarck for a brief visit, Alan and I drove to Maddock. It had now been sixteen years since we had sold our house and auctioned off most of the furniture. However, we had saved a few things that the new owners had allowed us to store in their attic. Planning to add more insulation to the attic, they had asked us to collect our belongings.

Alan and I arrived on August 19, the birthday of Dad and Ansel. We celebrated by taking Ansel and Dorothy out to eat. Returning home, we continued to visit, and then Alan and I headed upstairs to bed. We each crawled into our single beds, the same beds we had slept in after Mom died.

Alan went to sleep immediately, but I felt terribly restless. I tossed and turned as I thought back over all the years. I recalled vividly the pain I used to feel back in 1967 as I looked out the window at our house across the street. I had been grateful for a place to live, and yet I longed to be with Mom and Dad in "our home."

I also remembered how "homeless" I felt back then— feeling like the best part of my life was gone, facing an unknown future, a future I had to live without Mom and Dad. I felt the same way again. After sixteen years, I was back at square one in a sense: again facing an unknown future, again facing it without Mom and Dad.

But now I also had to face the future without Pauline. So many of the dreams I used to contemplate in that bed had come true. I had found someone to love, and I had been loved. I had found a marital bliss and beauty and depth even beyond what I had imagined those long years ago.

But now all that was gone, and I felt such a mysterious sorrow and restlessness as I lay their contemplating my present life.

I had to get up. I went into the adjoining bedroom with its double bed. This was the room Pauline and I stayed in whenever we came to visit.

I looked at everything in the room, and then sat on the bed, remembering all the times Pauline and I had been in that room together. Then the tears began. No loud wailing or sobbing. Just a quiet, steady stream of tears.

Somehow I felt more comfortable in that room. There I was reminded of the loss of Pauline. In the other room I felt the loss of all three. In that room I finally lay down, and fell soundly asleep.

The next morning Alan and I began unpacking the attic: music albums, toys, games, baby clothes, pictures, and my baseball card and marble collections. I had forgotten so many of those items, but they all brought back memories of those days so long ago. We saved many items, and threw others away. Another reminder of just how final death is.

That evening, as I headed back to Bismarck, I stopped at the cemetery. I needed to go to Mom's and Dad's graves. How long had it been? How many years? I couldn't remember, but I knew it had been a long time.

You see, I had avoided going to their graves. I never really understood why; I just knew I didn't want to go. "Well," I used to say, as my excuse, "Mom and Dad aren't there anyway."

That always surprised Pauline. In fact, I don't believe I ever took her to the graves of my parents. It was only shortly before Pauline's death that I began to understand why. It was because of the guilt I felt towards Dad and the anger I felt towards Mom. I didn't want to feel either, face either, and so I never wanted to go to the cemetery where I would have to confront those feelings.

As Pauline lay in the hospital dying, it dawned on me that I would have to decide where to bury her. That is when I asked her if I could bury her near me, telling her that I knew that I would need to go to her grave again and again.

Now, here I was at the cemetery in Maddock. I walked slowly to the "Erickson" headstone, then to the foot of the graves, side by side. Edrei A., 1911-1965, Ruth L., 1917-1967. I stood there, remembering what they looked like. There were no tears. Just a mysterious sense of loss, of loneliness. Then I began to circle their graves, and as I did I said, "I am making the circle of love that I made so many times around Pauline's grave. You never met Pauline, but you would have loved her. And she loved both of you very much."

I looked at the sky, at the setting sun, and then back at Maddock, the home of my childhood—the place I grew up, learned how to walk, learned how to read, learned how to swim, was baptized, confirmed and ordained. The place where I had dreamed, the place where I had hoped.

I looked down at the graves. "Goodbye Mom, goodbye Dad. I love you."

I walked to my car. I drove away. Down the road again. Striking out on a new journey. Not knowing where I would go, but knowing I must go. No longer innocent, no longer naïve. But also no longer broken, no longer on the verge of emotional death.

A strange peace came over me. For months I had been saying goodbye to Pauline. I had needed to say goodbye to Mom and Dad again, and now I had done that. Goodbye to so many belongings, goodbye to our old house, goodbye to my room in the Haukness home, goodbye at my parents' graves.

Years before I had headed down that highway, trusting God that it would be okay, that I would find meaning and fulfillment in my life. That had come true. There had been much struggle, much confusion, much pain, much work, but it had come true.

Now it was time to strike out again. The peace came as I realized that there was no reason why I could not hope again, dream again, trust again. I had been changed. I was a different man. I had another large hole in my heart. But I was still me, I was still loved, I still had a purpose, I still had the ability to dream, to hope, to trust.

There was no great joy. No laughter. No overwhelming feeling of happiness. But there also was not a deep, cutting, agonizing pain. Just a quiet, irenic calm. Just a peaceful feeling of security, warm in the remembrance of how much I had been loved, secure in the knowledge that I was still loved, by family, by so many gracious friends, by God.

I did not die in the Valley. By grace, I had been brought through. It wasn't Sunday quite yet. But I could feel, and soon see, the sun rising on a new day, a renewed life. I knew deep down that I was not alone. Jesus' parting words to his loved ones brought great comfort to me, and now those words included Dad, Mom and Pauline: ""Remember, I am with you always."' [Matthew 28:20b]

Epilogue   Resurrection and New Life

If the only prayer you said was thank you, that would be enough.
  --Meister Eckhart

"We are hoping you will return, along with other former pastors, to help us celebrate this important anniversary in the life of our congregation." It was early in 1994 and the letter came from Trinity Lutheran Church in Hemet, California, the congregation I was serving when Pauline died. I had not been back since departing for graduate school eleven years earlier.

I was now serving a congregation in Fargo, North Dakota. I was married to Mary, whom I had met within a month of driving down the road out of Maddock. We dated for less than a year, and were married in June 1984. We now had two children: Brian John Edrei, 8 years old, and Jessica Lynn, 4 years old.

A part of me wanted to make an excuse about why I could not go to the celebration. I didn't know if I was ready to face the pain and loss again. Another part of me wanted to return, with my entire family, so they could see first hand my new life.

Mary wasn't at all sure she wanted to go. Who could blame her? Would the members of Trinity receive her warmly? Did she want to face so directly the pain of my past? Perhaps it was best to just leave that part of my life undisturbed, much like a picture album put on a shelf and allowed to gather dust as the years pass by.

Reflecting on whether to return, I began to feel pulled towards doing so, but I really wanted to bring Mary with me. During this period of indecision Mary told a friend about her struggle, and the friend encouraged her to go with me, pointing out that this was an opportunity for Mary to be able to learn about an important part of my life that was at that point shrouded in mystery.

Meanwhile I decided to try to make the trip about more than just the church anniversary. We would fly into Los Angeles and visit my brother, Paul Haukness, and his family. Then we would drive south on the beautiful Pacific Coast Highway to spend a day in San Diego. From there we would go to Temecula for wine tasting before arriving in Hemet.

That is exactly what we ended up doing, and it was wonderful. However, once we left Temecula for Hemet a strange sadness began to build within me. What would it be like to face this place filled with so many painful memories?

Arriving in Hemet, we drove around town and I showed Mary where Pauline and I had lived, the church I had served and some of our favorite places to frequent. Then we went to Jack and Debbie Simmons house, where we would stay for the weekend. Jack had been a pallbearer at Pauline's funeral, and he and Debbie had been such good friends to Pauline and me and a wonderful support for me the year after Pauline died.

Arriving at the Simmons home, we were greeted with amazing warmth by a gathering of so many of our friends from a decade before. I knew immediately that we had made the right decision to return.

The next morning, Saturday, I invited Mary to visit Pauline's grave with me. I asked Jack and Debbie to remind me where the grave was in the cemetery and Mary drove me there, dropping me off as she went to buy flowers.

I couldn't remember exactly where the gravesite was. The trees were so much larger than when I had left Hemet and I immediately had trouble finding my bearings. In fact, when Mary returned with the flowers, I still couldn't find the grave. How typical of life! Just when we are trying to make an event special and sacred, reality sets in to disrupt our well-intentioned plans. All Mary and I could do was smile as she joined me in the search.

Finally I found the grave and its stone: "Pauline Marie Peterson Erickson, 1950-1982. I have fought the good fight. I have finished the race. I have kept the faith."

I introduced Mary to Pauline and she placed the flowers on the grave. I shared with Mary how I had spent so much time in this place the year after Pauline had died, making the "circle of love" I had done countless times that year.

That afternoon was spent at Trinity attending various anniversary events, including a wonderful gathering with the young adults who had been part of the youth program when I was at Trinity. Mary continued to meet congregational members, all of whom welcomed her with great warmth.

Finally it was time for the evening banquet at which each former pastor would have a few minutes to share a reflection. When it was my turn, I stood up and began:

> Hello. My name is Brian Erickson. I was a pastor here for only a brief time, from 1981 to 1983. This is my wife, Mary. We were married 10 years ago in 1984. We have two children, Brian John Edrei, age 8, and Jessica Lynn, age 4. I am now Senior Pastor at Peace Lutheran Church in Fargo, North Dakota.

> When I was your pastor I was in many ways a broken man. The first year here, as Pauline was dying, I was a man filled with constant fear. The second year here, after Pauline died, I was a man filled with great sorrow, struggling to deal with my grief.

> I returned for this anniversary because I wanted to thank you from the depths of my heart for the love and support you gave Pauline and me as she was dying, and the love and support you surrounded me with the year after she died.

The second reason I returned is to testify to God's resurrection power. In one of Pauline's last journal entries, written on the Easter before she died, she talked about Easter weekend as a microcosm of life: Good Friday is a time of despair, desolation, heartbreak, hell and death; Saturday is a time of loneliness and grief; Sunday is a time of joy, happiness and life anew!

When I left Trinity, it was still Saturday in my life. I returned now because I want to testify to the Easter Pauline wrote about. God took me from grief and death to a new life filled again with love and purpose. You were a large part of that resurrection power, but it was far from complete when I left here. Thank you for standing with me, and thank you for testifying to God's power to take us when we are lifeless and breathe the spirit of new life and hope back into our broken bodies and spirits.

May God continue to bless you and this congregation on your journey to bring healing and hope to all those places and people where there is loss and grief. You have been for me the embodiment of the promise of God spoken through the prophet Jeremiah: "For surely I know the plans I have for you, says the Lord, plans for your welfare and not for harm, to give you a future with hope." [Jeremiah 29:11; NRSV]

Dedication II

This book is dedicated to Mary Jane, Brian John Edrei and Jessica Lynn. I may have found new life without you, but it would have been a life with so much less joy, fun, adventure, love, purpose and meaning.

Made in the USA
Columbia, SC
13 July 2019